Communization and its Discontents:
Contestation, Critique, and Contemporary Struggles

Communization and its Discontents: Contestation, Critique, and Contemporary Struggles
Edited by Benjamin Noys

ISBN 978-1-57027-231-8

Released by Minor Compositions, Wivenhoe / New York / Port Watson

Minor Compositions is a series of interventions & provocations drawing from autonomous politics, avant-garde aesthetics, and the revolutions of everyday life.

Minor Compositions is an imprint of Autonomedia
www.minorcompositions.info | minorcompositions@gmail.com

Distributed by Autonomedia
PO Box 568 Williamsburgh Station
Brooklyn, NY 11211

Phone/fax: 718-963-0568
www.autonomedia.org
info@autonomedia.org

Cover and layout by mark@alphabetthreat.co.uk

Communization and its Discontents:
Contestation, Critique, and Contemporary Struggles

Edited by Benjamin Noys

The Fabric of Struggles
Benjamin Noys

I

Barely twenty years have passed since the collapse of actually-existing so-cialism and now the crisis of actually-existing capitalism, in its neoliberal version, is upon us. The shrill capitalist triumphalism of the 1990s, or the bellicose equation of capitalism with democracy that defined the '00s 'war on terror', ring more than a little hollow in the frozen desert of burst fi-nancial bubbles and devalorization. The commodities that make up the capitalist way-of-life have turned malignant, exposed as hollow bearers of debt servitude that can never be paid off. The cry 'No New Deal' goes up as wealth is transferred in huge amounts to save the financial sector. We are prepared for yet another round of sacrifice as structural adjustment and 'shock doctrine' return to the center of global capitalism after exten-sive testing on its self-defined 'peripheries'. Whether this is terminal crisis, entropic drift, or merely the prelude to the 'creative destruction' that will kick-start a new round of accumulation, is still obscure.

In this situation new waves and forms of struggle have emerged in dispersed and inchoate forms. We have also seen a new language being used to theorise and think these struggles: 'the human strike', the 'imaginary party', 'clandestinity' and, not least, the strange and spectral word 'communization'. The concept of communization emerged from currents of the French ultra-left in the late 1960s and early 1970s, but has gained resonance as a way of posing the problem of struggle today. It draws attention to the exhaustion of existing forms of organization that have tried to lead, dictate or pre-empt struggles, it contests the tendency to affirm or adopt an alternative counter-identity (worker, militant, anarchist, activist, etc.), and it challenges the despotism of capitalism that treats us as sources of value.

II

This collection is dedicated to a critical questioning of the concept of communization, and in particular to analysing its discontents – the problems, questions and difficulties that traverse it. It is not easy to define what the word communization refers to, and it has often been used more as a slogan, a nickname, or even worse a 'brand', than forces together very different perspectives and analyses. What we find 'in' communization is often a weird mixing-up of insurrectionist anarchism, the communist ultra-left, post-autonomists, anti-political currents, groups like the Invisible Committee, as well as more explicitly 'communizing' currents, such as Théorie Communiste and Endnotes. Obviously at the heart of the word is *communism* and, as the shift to communization suggests, communism as a particular *activity* and *process*, but what that is requires some further exploration.

Here I want to give some initial points of orientation, which are explored further in the contributions that follow, by analyzing the communizing arguments that pose struggle as *immediate*, *immanent*, and as *anti-identity*. In each case I want to treat these points as sites of dispute, especially between the theorisations of the well-known contemporary French radical grouping associated with the journal *Tiqqun*, also publishing under the name 'The Invisible Committee' (henceforth I will refer to them as 'Tiqqun' for convenience), on the one hand, and the less-known but explicitly communizing currents of Théorie Communiste (TC) and Endnotes, on the other.

What does it mean to say that communization is or should be immediate? It suggests there is no transition to communism, no stage of socialism required before we can achieve the stage of communism, and so no need to 'build' communism. This, however, has a very different meaning in different hands. For Tiqqun and others influenced by anarchist prefigurative politics this immediacy means that we must begin enacting communism *now*, within capitalism. From the commune to 'commoning', from cyber-activism to new 'forms-of-life', in this perspective we can't make any transition to communism but must live it as a reality now to ensure its eventual victory. On the other hand, TC and Endnotes give this 'immediacy' a rather different sense, by arguing that communization implies the immediacy of communism in the process of revolution. In fact, they are deeply suspicious of a prefigurative or alternative politics, regarding such forms of struggle as mired in capitalism and often moralistic.[1] Instead, if anything, contemporary struggles can only be *negatively* prefigurative, indicating the limits of our forms of struggle and indicating only possible new lines of attack.

These differences are also reflected in the posing of the communization in terms of immanence. The point here is that communization requires that we start thinking communism from *within* the immanent conditions of global capitalism rather than from a putatively radical or communist 'outside', but again this can lead in very different directions. Tiqqun regard capitalism as globally dominant, but also see it as leaving spaces and times through which revolt can emerge, or into which revolt can slip away from power. They regard capitalism as porous or, in Deleuze and Guattari's formulation, 'holey'.[2] This kind of 'enclave' theory is a familiar strategy, ranging from the Italian social centers, to squats, to communal gardening, communes themselves, and other practices of 'commoning'. This kind of formulation appeals to struggles in progress, to activists, and so links with the claim for a prefigurative immediacy. Again we might not be surprised to see that TC and Endnotes disagree. They too regard capitalism as dominant, but as a contradictory totality fissured by class struggles between proletariat and capital. There is no 'outside', or 'line of flight', but only a thinking through of this immanent contradiction and antagonism secreted within capitalist exploitation of labor to extract value.

In terms of the contesting of 'identity', Tiqqun develop a new clandestine or 'invisible' identity of the militant that escapes capitalist control and capture. Refusing the 'old' identity models of Marxism, the working class or proletariat, as well as the 'new' models of identity politics, they instead prefer the language of contemporary theory: 'whatever singularities', or post-identity models that intimate new 'forms-of-life'. In contrast TC and Endnotes retain the classical Marxist language of the proletariat, but insist that this is not an identity, but rather a mode of self-abolishing. We cannot reinforce a 'workers' identity', or try to replace this with another identity. Instead, the negativity of the proletariat consists in the fact it can only operate by abolishing itself.

III

If there are disagreements in the forms which the analysis of struggle should take there seems to be initial agreement about what communization opposes: capitalism. Again, however, this is often a point of contention. Many in the communizing current adopt a variant of Marx's distinction, from the unpublished sixth chapter of capital the 'Results of the Immediate Process of Production',[3] between formal and real subsumption. Formal subsumption is the general form of capitalist domination, and involves capital subsuming an existing form of production 'as it finds it'. For example, peasants may still work in the fields in the way they always have but now they are compelled to take their goods to market to realise value. In this mode of subsumption, Marx argues, capital generates absolute surplus-value, and can only do so by demanding extension to the working day. So, surplus-value can only be generated by forcing work beyond the amount necessary for self-reproduction, although this compulsion does not tend to happen directly but through economic functions, i.e. you need to produce a surplus to generate income to live, rather than to pay off a feudal lord. This stands in contrast to real subsumption, in which capital revolutionizes the actual mode of labor to produce the specifically capitalist mode of production. Here compulsion increases relative surplus-value by the use of machinery, the intensification of labor and the remaking of the production process. It is real subsumption which produces a truly capitalist mode of production.

Within communization, and especially for TC, Marx's distinction is often taken as a model of historical periodization. While Marx, and others like Endnotes, see formal and real subsumption as intertwined processes that have developed with capitalism and take different forms,[4] the periodizing argument suggests that we have shifted from formal subsumption to real subsumption. In the argument of TC this shift is linked to cycles of struggle. In the initial phase of capitalist accumulation we have formal subsumption, and class struggle expresses itself in the affirmation of a pre-capitalist identity and 'moral economy'.[5] With the advance of real subsumption, in the industrial form of the factory during the latter half of the 19th century, we see a new antagonism of the worker versus capitalism, which reaches its apogee in the Russian Revolution. In this new cycle of struggles central is the independent workers' identity, and TC call this form of struggle 'programmatism'. Here the forms of struggle actually become 'internal' to capitalism, as the relation becomes mediated through unions, social welfare, and other forms of Keynesian control. These 'revolutions' tend to reinforce capitalism, encouraging the passage from formal to real subsumption through 'socialist accumulation', and lead to the theology of labor and the oxymoron of the 'workers' state'. This 'programmatism' comes into crisis with the struggles of the 1960s and 1970s, when workers now abolish their identities and flee the factory. The extension of real subsumption over life, what Italian autonomists called the 'social factory', generalises struggles. In the capitalist counter-attack, however, we witness a second phase of real subsumption, a re-making of the world in the conformity to capital and the crisis of the identity of the 'worker'. This re-making was, of course, central to the project of neoliberalism.[6]

Such an analysis is shared by Jacques Camatte, Antonio Negri, and many other post-autonomists. It could seem to imply the pessimistic conclusion that 'resistance is futile', that capitalism is a monstrous alien subject that vampirically draws all of life within itself (to mix Marx's gothic metaphors). Such a position was visible in the Frankfurt school's positing of a 'totally-administered' or 'one-dimensional' society. It is taken today by certain currents of primitivism or anti-civilization anarchism, which desperately try to recover the few remaining fragments of 'non-capitalist' life and backdate the origins of oppression to the Neolithic agricultural revolution, or even to the origin of language itself. Communization, in contrast, regards the passage to the dominance of real subsumption as requiring and generating new forms of struggle and antagonism that entail the abandoning of the affirmation of the worker and 'workers' power'.

Again, differences emerge at this point. Negri and the post-autonomists tend to argue for the emergence of the power of the 'multitude', which is always ready to burst through the capitalist integument and install communism Tiqqun stress new 'singularities' or 'forms-of-life', which escape or flee or declare war on the forms and structures of real subsumption TC argue for new self-abolishing relations of struggle as the contradictions sharpen and the 'proletariat' is no longer a viable identity in capitalism and so communism only really becomes possible now Gilles Dauvé and Karl Nesic prefer to see communization as an immanent possibility of struggles across the history of capitalism, an invariant of the capitalist mode of production,[7] while Endnotes accept the diagnosis of the crisis of programmatism, but reject the bluntness of the periodization of subsumption by TC and others.

Without wishing to collapse these important differences we can see the emphasis on the 'horizon' of capitalism as dominant, even in the moment of crisis. It is capitalism that forms the terrain and 'fabric of struggles' which communization tries to engage with and theorise. It is also class struggle and capitalist responses to that struggle that have re-posed the crisis of the workers' movement and pose the need to create new modes of thinking contemporary struggles. That said, how we think and understand the form and history of capitalism is a crucial point of debate to develop forms of struggle against it, and different understandings lead to very different conclusions.

IV

I want to baldly state some of the interconnected problems that seem to immediately face communization as a theory. The first is that the final collapse of actually-existing socialism in 1989, and the widespread disenchantment with social democracy, unions, and other 'traditional' affirmations of the worker as means of resistance, does not seem, as yet, to have led to any rebound to a self-abolishing model of proletarian negativity or the 'multitude', or 'whatever singularities', or other 'new' modes of struggle. While 'programmatism' is obviously in crisis a replacement is not evident. Of course, it could always be argued that these forms of struggle are still emerging, still nascent, or that their lack of appearance is a sign of a transition beyond 'programmatism', but in the context of capitalist crisis, and capitalist-induced ecological crisis, this doesn't seem to offer much reassurance. While the workers' states were often terrible and bloody failures, not least for the working class, the emergence of an alternative 'real movement' is hard to detect to say the least. Even the austerity of the TC position, which prefers to only negatively trace 'emergent' forms of struggle and their limits, still depends on a minimal teleology that implies new forms of possible revolution, and so still has to confront this problem.

A second problem, which I've already noted in passing, is that the triumph of 'real subsumption', which integrates the reproduction of the proletariat to the self-reproduction of capital, seems to allow very little space, or time, for resistance. Even if we don't think in terms of real subsumption, but rather the global dominance of capitalism or 'Empire', we still have to confront the issue of whether it can be defeated, and how. The ways in which capitalism permeates and modulates the whole of life (what Deleuze called 'the society of control'[8]) leaves us with little leverage to resist. In particular the end of the 'workers' standpoint', the end of the classical proletariat, seems to deprive us of an agency to make the mass changes communization would require. While TC insists on the proletariat as conceptual marker, they have to struggle with its empirical non-emergence.[9] The alternative articulations of possible agents of change, such as immaterial workers or 'whatever singularities', by other currents of communization are very thinly-specified.

This leads to a third problem. While communization insists on immediacy and the abandonment of debates about 'transition' or teleology, i.e. debates on what we are aiming to achieve, it's hard to see how it can coordinate or develop such 'moments' of communization globally across the social field (as it would have to, to destroy or counter a global capitalism). This is true for those who emphasise communizing now, in which case how do such moments come together and avoid remaining merely 'alternative'? It is also true if we regard communizing as intrinsic to revolution, because then we must answer how the process of communizing can be coordinated in a revolution that will be a geographically and temporally striated, dispersed and differential? TC pose this question when they ask: 'How can a "unity" arise, in a general movement of class struggle, that is not in fact a unity but an inter-activity?', their unsatisfactory answer: 'We do not know... But class struggle has often showed us its infinite inventiveness.'[10] Pending proof of this 'inventiveness', there is a risk that communization becomes a valorization of only fleeting moments of revolt, of small chinks in which the light of revolution penetrates capitalist darkness; or that it become the promise of a total revolution that will achieve its aim in process, without any substantial account of how that might take place. This is not to call for a return to the 'party' form, or to rehash debates concerning Leninism (debates that might well be important), but rather to suggest that the difficulty in specifying agents of change can also flow into the difficulties in specifying the contents of change. Certainly, communization was right to critique the formalism of the left, what TC calls its 'programmatism', that could only ever argue that once we had the correct form (Leninist party, workers' councils, etc.) communism would unfold. What is as yet unclear is what forms of struggle will make 'the poetry of the future'.

These are, of course, not only problems for communization, but for any attempts to make radical change. What I want to stress is the acuity with which communization allows us to pose these problems, and the stress it places on engaging with them, rather than presuming they will be dissolved in some rush to 'praxis'. Communization as a problematic links together issues of the current state of struggle, and their seeming 'disappearance' in traditional forms, the nature of capitalism and the possible agents who might resist this social formation, and the strategic or tactical forms that resistance might or will take. It is to the necessity of thinking and theorizing these problems and others in the light of 'communization' that this collection is devoted.

V

The chapters, or better interventions, which follow, speak for themselves, and certainly, and deliberately, they do not speak in the same voice. If communization is a way of stating a problem then there is no requirement for agreement on what that problem is, or even agreement that communization is the best way of posing it. Also, of course, this collection itself is in process – it is certainly not exhaustive, what collection could be?, and it doesn't aim at closure. But I do want to provide some general indications of the 'drift', to use the word in the Situationist sense, of these interventions.

We begin with the 'moment of communization' – a series of texts that frame the competing definitions of communization, and especially the conflict between those associated with TC/Endnotes and Tiqqun. Through the sharpening and analysis of these contrasts it becomes possible to assess the nature and originality of the communizing hypothesis. The next section is 'Frames of Struggle', which deals with how we conceptualize our contemporary political situation and how we conceptualize capitalism itself. The aim here is to reflect on the problem of the contemporary forms of capitalism, and to assess how we might understand the horizon of a seemingly 'totalitarian' capitalism, especially of capitalism in crisis, alongside the unevenness of capitalist power. The section 'Strategies of Struggle' considers how communization has drawn on and re-tooled 'traditional' modes of struggle, especially the 'barricade', the commons and the question of revolutionary violence. Again, it is in the re-working of more familiar concepts that we can assess the originality of the communizing hypothesis. Finally, the section 'No Future?' takes the slogan that was common to both punk and neoliberalism and turns it into a question. This is the question of the possible futures of the project of communization in regards to two key areas of our contemporary situation: the problem of gender / sexuality, and the problem of the new models and forms of digital practice. The aim of this section, and the collection as a whole, is not to provide a new reified recipe book for revolution, but rather to pose as a problem the kinds and forms of political (or non-political, or anti-political) action that are possible today.

VI

In his story 'The Two Kings and the Two Labyrinths' Jorge Luis Borges describes the competition between two kings to construct the perfect, and so impossible to escape, labyrinth or maze.[11] The first king uses the traditional method of constructing a highly-complex series of tunnels, resulting in a terrible labyrinth which the second king only escapes from by the intervention of God. In his turn the second king lays waste to the first king's lands and casts him into a labyrinth impossible to defeat: the desert. The impossibility of this labyrinth lies not in the choice of paths, but the absence of any paths. For Tiqqun we are living the 'deepening of the desert', the neutralisation of means to orient ourselves and escape the 'labyrinth' of capital.[12] This certainly overstates the case. Capitalism is not a 'featureless' terrain or 'smooth space', but in its combined and uneven development, including in the moment of globalized crisis, it is proving to be a labyrinth that is hard to traverse. Communization is not our compass, and this collection does not exhaustively map this labyrinth. Many other paths are possible, in fact in the desert we face not so much a 'garden of forking paths' but the infinite multiplicity of paths we cannot even yet trace. So, this collection is merely, but essentially, a posing of the problem. To start to find what paths there might be, to not accept the (capitalist) desert as 'natural' phenomenon, and to begin to detect the struggles that will (re) make this terrain.

The Moment of Communization

What are we to do?
Endnotes

The term 'communization' has recently become something of a buzzword. A number of factors have contributed to this, the most prominent being the coming into fashion of various texts. Of these, *The Coming Insurrection* – associated with the French journal *Tiqqun*, and the 'Tarnac 9' who gained the doubtful prestige of being at the center of a major 'terrorist' scandal – has been by far the most influential. In addition to this, the voluble literature produced by autumn 2009's wave of Californian student struggles – a literature partly inspired by such French texts – has been a significant factor.[13] The confluence in this Californian literature of, on the one hand, a language inflected by typically grandiloquent Tiqqunisms, and on the other, concepts in part derived from the works of a more Marxist French ultra-left – and the convenient presence in both of these reference points of a fairly unusual term, 'communization' – has contributed to the appearance of a somewhat mythological discourse around this word. This communization appears as a fashionable stand-in for slightly more venerable buzzwords such as 'autonomy', having at least the sparkle of something new to it, a frisson of radical immediatism, and the support of some eloquent-sounding French literature. This communization is, if anything, a vague new incarnation of the simple idea that the revolution is something that we must do *now, here, for ourselves,* gelling nicely with the sentiments of an already-existent insurrectionist anarchism.

But this communization is, in all but the most abstract sense, something other than that which has been debated for some thirty years amongst the obscure communist groups who have lent the most content to this term, even if it bears traces of its ancestors' features, and may perhaps be illuminated by their theories. Of course, 'communization' was never the private property of such-and-such groups. It has, at least, a certain minor place in the general lexicon of left-wing tradition as a process of rendering communal or common. Recently some have begun to speak, with similar intended meaning, of ongoing processes of 'commonization'. But such general concepts are not interesting in themselves; if we were to attempt to divine some common content in the clutter of theories and practices grouped under such terms, we would be left with only the thinnest abstraction. We will thus concern ourselves here only with the two usages of the word that are at stake in the current discourse of communization: that derived from texts such as *The Coming Insurrection*, and that derived from writings by Troploin, Théorie Communiste and other post-68 French communists. It is primarily from these latter writings – those of Théorie Communiste (TC) in particular – that we derive our own understanding of communization, an understanding which we will sketch in what follows. As it happens, these two usages both proliferated from France into Anglophone debates in recent years, a process in which we have played a part. But it would be a mistake to take this coincidence for the sign of a single French debate over communization, or of a continuous 'communizationist' tendency within which the authors of *The Coming Insurrection* and, for example, TC represent divergent positions. What is common to these usages at most, is that they can be said to signal a certain insistence on immediacy in thinking about how a communist revolution happens. But, as we shall see, one 'immediate' is not the same as another; the question is which mediations are absent?

If the tone of the following text is often polemical, this is not because we take pleasure in criticising people already subject to a very public manhandling by the French state, charged as 'terrorists' on the meagre basis of allegations that they wrote a book and committed a minor act of sabotage. It is because long-running debates related to the concept of communization – debates in which we have participated – have become falsely associated with the theories presented in texts such as *The Coming Insurrection* and *Call*, and are thereby in danger of getting lost in the creeping fog that these texts have summoned.[14] What is at stake is not only these texts, but the Anglophone reception of 'communization' in general. It has thus become necessary to make the distinction: the 'communization theory' now spoken of in the Anglosphere is largely an imaginary entity, an artefact of the Anglophone reception of various unrelated works. The limited availability of relevant works in English, and the near-simultaneity with which some of these works became more widely known, surely contributed to the confusion; a certain traditional predisposition in relation to France, its theory and politics, probably helped. The Anglosphere has a peculiar tendency to take every crowing of some Gallic cock as a cue to get busy in the potting shed with its own theoretical confabulations; add to this a major political scandal, and it seems it is practically unable to contain the excitement.

But our intention is not simply to polemicize from the standpoint of some alternative theory. Insofar as it is possible to grasp the determinate circumstances which produce texts like this, they do not simply present *incorrect* theories. They present rather, the partial, broken fragments of a historical moment grasped in thought. In attempting to hold fast to the general movement of the capitalist class relation, communist theory may shed light on the character of such moments, and thereby the theoretical constructs which they produce. And, in so doing, it may also expose their limits, elisions and internal contradictions. Insofar as such constructs are symptomatic of the general character of the historical moment, their interrogation may draw out something about the character of the class relation as a whole.

If communization signals a certain immediacy in *how the revolution happens*, for us this does not take the form of a practical prescription; 'communization' does not imply some injunction to start making the revolution *right away*, or on an individual basis. What is most at stake, rather, is the question of *what the revolution is*; 'communization' is the name of an answer to this question. The content of such an answer necessarily depends on what is to be overcome: that is, the self-reproduction of the capitalist class relation, and the complex of social forms which are implicated in this reproduction – value-form, capital, gender distinction, state form, legal form, etc. In particular, such an overcoming must necessarily be the direct self-abolition of the working class, since anything short of this leaves capital with its obliging partner, ready to continue the dance of accumulation. Communization signifies the process of this direct self-abolition, and it is in the *directness* of this self-abolition that communization can be said to signify a certain 'immediacy'.

Communization is typically opposed to a traditional notion of the transitional period which was always to take place *after* the revolution, when the proletariat would be able to realise communism, having already taken hold of production and/ or the state. Setting out on the basis of the continued existence of the working class, the transitional period places the real revolution on a receding horizon, meanwhile perpetuating that which it is supposed to overcome. For us this is not a strategic question, since these matters have been settled by historical developments – the end of the programmatic workers' movement, the disappearance of positive working class identity, the absence of any kind of workers' power on the horizon: it is no longer possible to imagine a transition to communism on the basis of a prior victory of the working class *as* working class. To hold to council-ist or Leninist conceptions of revolution now is utopian, measuring reality against mental constructs which bear no historical actuality. The class struggle has outlived programmatism, and different shapes now inhabit its horizon. With the growing superfluity of the working class to production – its tendential reduction to a mere surplus population – and the resultantly tenuous character of the wage form as the essential meeting point of the twin circuits of reproduction, it can only be delusional to conceive revolution in terms of workers' power. Yet it is still the working class which must abolish itself.[15]

For us, communization does not signify some general positive process of 'sharing' or 'making common'. It signifies the specific revolutionary undoing of the relations of property constitutive of the capitalist class relation. Sharing *as such* – if this has any meaning at all – can hardly be understood as involving this undoing of capitalist relations, for various kinds of 'sharing' or 'making common' can easily be shown to play important roles within capitalist society without in any way impeding capitalist accumulation. Indeed, they are often essential to – or even constitutive in – that accumulation: consumption goods shared within families, risk shared via insurance, resources shared within firms, scientific knowledge shared through academic publications, standards and protocols shared between rival capitals because they are recognized as being in their common interest. In such cases, without contradiction, what is held in common is the counterpart to an appropriation. As such, a dynamic of communization would involve the undoing of such forms of 'sharing', just as it would involve the undoing of private appropriation. And while some might valorize a sharing that facilitates a certain level of subsistence beyond what the wage enables, in a world dominated by the reproduction of the capitalist class relation such practices can occur only at the margins of this reproduction, as alternative or supplementary means of survival, and as such, they are not revolutionary in themselves.

Communization is a movement at the level of the totality, through which that totality is abolished. The logic of the movement that abolishes this totality necessarily differs from that which applies at the level of the concrete individual or group: it should go without saying that no individual or group can overcome the reproduction of the capitalist class relation through their own actions. The determination of an individual act as 'communizing' flows only from the overall movement of which it is part, not from the act itself, and it would therefore be wrong to think of the revolution in terms of the sum of already-communizing acts, as if all that was needed was a certain accumulation of such acts to a critical point. A conception of the revolution as such an accumulation is premised on a quantitative extension which is supposed to provoke a qualitative transformation. In this it is not unlike the problematic of the *growing-over* of everyday struggles into revolution which was one of the salient characteristics of the programmatic epoch.[16] In contrast to these linear conceptions of revolution, communization is the product of a qualitative shift within the dynamic of class struggle itself. Communization occurs only at the limit of a struggle, in the rift that opens as this struggle meets its limit and is pushed beyond it. Communization thus has little positive advice to give us about particular, immediate practice in the here and now, and it certainly cannot prescribe particular skills, such as lock-picking or bone-setting, as so many roads, by which insurrectionary subjects to heaven go.[17] What advice it can give is primarily negative: the social forms implicated in the reproduction of the capitalist class relation will not be instruments of the revolution, since they are part of that which is to be abolished.

Communization is thus not a form of *prefigurative* revolutionary practice of the sort that diverse anarchisms aspire to be, since it does not have any positive existence prior to a revolutionary situation. While it is possible to see the question of communization as in some sense posed by the dynamic of the present capitalist class relation, communization does not yet appear directly as a form of practice, or as some set of individuals with the right ideas about such practice. This does not mean that we should merely *await* communization as some sort of messianic arrival – in fact, this is not an option, for engagement in the dynamic of the capitalist class relation is not something that can be opted out of, nor into, for that matter. Involvement in the class struggle is not a matter of a political practice which can be arbitrarily chosen, from a contemplative standpoint. Struggles demand our participation, even though they do not yet present themselves as *the revolution*. The theory of communization alerts us to the limits inherent in such struggles, and indeed it is attentive to the possibilities of a real revolutionary rupture opening up because of, rather than in spite of, these limits. For us then, communization is an answer to the question of what the revolution is. This is a question which takes a specific historical form in the face of the self-evident bankruptcy of the old programmatic notions, leftist, anarchist, and ultra-leftist alike: how will the overcoming of the capitalist class relation take place, given that it is impossible for the proletariat to affirm itself as a class yet we are still faced with the problem of this relation? Texts such as *Call* or *The Coming Insurrection* however, do not even properly ask the question of *what the revolution is*, for in these texts the problem has already been evaporated into a conceptual miasma. In these texts, the revolution will be made not by any existing class, or on the basis of any real material, historical situation; it will be made by 'friendships', by 'the formation of sensibility as a force', 'the deployment of an archipelago of worlds', 'an other side of reality', 'the party of insurgents' – but most of all by that ever-present and always amorphous positivity: *we*. The reader is beseeched to take sides with this 'we' – the 'we *of a position*' – to join it in the imminent demise of 'capitalism, civilization, empire, call it what you wish'. Instead of a concrete, contradictory relation, there are 'those who can hear' the call, and those who cannot; those who perpetuate 'the desert', and those with 'a disposition to forms of communication so intense that, when put into practice, they snatch from the enemy most of its force.' Regardless of their statements to the contrary,[18] do these pronouncements amount to anything more than the self-affirmations of a self-identifying radical milieu?

In this more insurrectionist incarnation, communization emerges as an answer to a real historical question. But the question in this case is the 'what should we do?' posed by the conclusion of the wave of struggles that had the anti-globalization movement at its center.[19] The authors correctly recognize the impossibility of developing any real autonomy to 'what is held in common' within capitalist society, yet the exhaustion of the summit-hopping, black-blocking activist milieu makes it imperative for them to either find new practices in which to engage, or to stage a graceful retreat. Thus the 'TAZ', the alternative, the commune etc., are to be re-thought, but with a critique of alternativism in mind: we must secede, yes, but this secession must also involve 'war'.[20] Since such supposedly liberated places cannot be stabilised as *outside* of 'capitalism, civilization, empire, call it what you wish', they are to be reconceived as part of the expansion and generalization of a broad insurrectionary struggle. Provided the struggle is successful, these alternatives will not turn out to have been impossible after all; their generalization is to be the condition of their possibility. It is this dynamic of generalization that is identified as one of 'communization' – communization as, more or less, the forming of communes in a process that doesn't stop until the problem of the alternative has been solved, since it no longer has to be an alternative. But all of this is without any clear notion of what is to be undone through such a dynamic. The complexity of actual social relations, and the real dynamic of the class relation, are dispatched with a showmanly flourish in favor of a clutch of vapid abstractions. Happy that the *we* of the revolution does not need any real definition, all that is to be overcome is arrogated to the *they* – an entity which can remain equally abstract: an ill-defined generic nobodaddy (capitalism, civilization, empire etc) that is to be undone by – at the worst points of *Call* – the Authentic Ones who have forged 'intense' friendships, and who still really *feel* despite the *badness* of the world.

But the problem cannot rest only with this 'they', thereby fundamentally exempting this 'we of a position' from the dynamic of revolution. On the contrary, in any actual supersession of the capitalist class relation *we ourselves* must be overcome; 'we' have no 'position' apart from the capitalist class relation. What we are is, at the deepest level, constituted by this relation, and it is a rupture with the reproduction of what we are that will necessarily form the horizon of our struggles. It is no longer possible for the working class to identify itself positively, to embrace its class character as the essence of what it is; yet it is still stamped with the simple facticity of its class belonging day by day as it faces, in capital, the condition of its existence. In this period, the 'we' of revolution does not affirm itself, does not identify itself positively, because it cannot; it cannot assert itself against the 'they' of capital without being confronted by the problem of its own existence – an existence which it will be the nature of the revolution to overcome. There is nothing to affirm in the capitalist class relation; no autonomy, no alternative, no outside, no secession.

An implicit premise of texts like *Call* and *The Coming Insurrection* is that, if our class belonging ever was a binding condition, it is no longer. Through an immediate act of assertion we can refuse such belonging here and now, position ourselves outside of the problem. It is significant perhaps that it is not only the milieu associated with *Tiqqun* and *The Coming Insurrection* that have developed theory which operates on this premise over the last decade. In texts such as *Communism of Attack and Communism of Withdrawal* Marcel, and the Batko group with which he is now associated, offer a much more sophisticated variant. Rather than the self-valorizations of an insurrectionist scene, in this case the theory emerges as a reconceived autonomism informed by a smorgasbord of esoteric theory – Marxian and otherwise – but ultimately the formal presuppositions are the same.[21] Taking the immanence of the self-reproduction of the class relation for a closed system without any conceivable terminus, Marcel posits the necessity of a purely external, transcendent moment – the 'withdrawal' on the basis of which communists can launch an 'attack'. But, within this world, what can such 'withdrawal' ever mean other than the voluntaristic forming of a kind of 'radical' milieu which the state is quite happy to tolerate as long as it refrains from expressing, in an attempt to rationalise its continued reproduction within capitalist society, the kind of combativity which we find in *The Coming Insurrection*?

To insist, against this, on the complete immanence of the capitalist class relation – on our complete entwinement with capital – is not to resign ourselves to a monolithic, closed totality, which can do nothing other than reproduce itself. Of course, it appears that way if one sets out from the assumption of the voluntaristically conceived subject: for such a subject, the totality of real social relations could only ever involve the mechanical unfolding of some purely *external* process. But this subject is a historically specific social form, itself perpetuated through the logic of the reproduction of the class relation, as is its complement. Not insensitive to the problem of this subject, *The Coming Insurrection* sets out with a disavowal of the Fichtean I=I which it finds exemplified in Reebok's 'I am what I am' slogan. The 'self' here is an imposition of the 'they'; a kind of neurotic, administered form which 'they mean to stamp upon us'.[22] The 'we' is to reject this imposition, and put in its place a conception of 'creatures among creatures, singularities among similars, living flesh weaving the flesh of the world'.[23] But the 'we' that rejects this imposition is still a voluntarist subject; its disavowal of the 'self' remains only a disavowal, and the replacement of this by more interesting-sounding terms does not get us out of the problem. In taking the imposition of the 'self' upon it to be something unidirectional and purely external, the 'we' posits another *truer* self beyond the first, a self which is truly its own. This authentic selfhood – 'singularity', 'creature', 'living flesh' – need not be individualistically conceived, yet it remains a voluntarist subject which grasps itself as self-standing, and the objectivity that oppresses it as merely something *over there*. The old abstraction of the egoistic subject goes through a strange mutation in the present phase in the form of the insurrectionist – a truly Stirnerite subject – for whom it is not only class belonging that can be cast off through a voluntarist assertion, but the very imposition of the 'self' *per se*. But while our class belonging

32

is unaffirmable – a mere condition of our being in our relation with capital – and while the abstract 'self' may be part of the totality which is to be superseded – this does not mean that either is voluntarily renounceable. It is only in the revolutionary undoing of this totality that these forms can be overcome.

The prioritisation of a certain *tactical* conception is a major outcome and determinant of this position. Theory is called upon to legitimate a practice which cannot be abandoned, and a dualism results: the voluntarist 'we', and the impassive objectivity which is its necessary counterpart. For all their claims to have overcome 'classical politics', these texts conceive the revolution ultimately in terms of two opposed lines: the we that 'gets organized', and all the forces arrayed against it. Tactical thought is then the guide and rule for this 'we', mediating its relations with an object which remains external. Instead of a theoretical reckoning with the concrete totality that must be overcome in all its determinations, or a reconstruction of the real horizon of the class relation, we get a sundering of the totality into two basic abstractions, and a simple set of exhortations and practical prescriptions whose real theoretical function is to bring these abstractions into relation once more. Of course, neither *Call* nor *The Coming Insurrection* present themselves straightforwardly as offering 'a theory'. *Call* in particular attempts to circumvent theoretical questions by appealing from the outset to 'the evident', which is 'not primarily a matter of logic or reasoning', but is rather that which 'attaches to the sensible, to *worlds*', that which is 'held in common' or 'sets apart'.[24] The ostensible point of these texts is to stage a simple *cri de coeur* – an immediate, pre-theoretical stocktaking of reasons for rebelling against this bad, bad world – on the basis of which people will join the authors in making the insurrection. But this proclamation of immediacy disguises a theory which has already done the mediating, which has pre-constructed the 'evident'; a theory whose founding commitments are to the 'we' that must *do something*, and to its paternal *they* – commitments which forestall any grasp of the real situation. Theory which substitutes for itself the simple description of *what we must do* fails

33

at its own task, since in renouncing its real standpoint as theory it gives up the prospect of actually understanding not only what is to be overcome, but also what this overcoming must involve.

Communist theory sets out not from the false position of some voluntarist subject, but from the posited supersession of the totality of forms which are implicated in the reproduction of this subject. As merely posited, this supersession is necessarily abstract, but it is only through this basic abstraction that theory takes as its content the determinate forms which are to be superseded; forms which stand out in their determinacy precisely because their dissolution has been posited. This positing is not only a matter of methodology, or some kind of necessary postulate of reason, for the supersession of the capitalist class relation is not a mere theoretical construct. Rather, it runs ahead of thought, being posited incessantly by this relation itself; it is its very horizon as an antagonism, the real negative presence which it bears. Communist theory is produced by – and necessarily thinks within – this antagonistic relation; it is thought *of* the class relation, and it grasps itself as such. It attempts to conceptually reconstruct the totality which is its ground, in the light of the already-posited supersession of this totality, and to draw out the supersession as it presents itself here. Since it is a relation which has no ideal 'homeostatic' state, but one which is always beyond itself, with capital facing the problem of labor at every turn – even in its victories – the adequate thought of this relation is not of some equilibrium state, or some smoothly self-positing totality; it is of a fundamentally *impossible* relation, something that is only insofar as it is ceasing to be; an internally unstable, antagonistic relation. Communist theory thus has no need of an external, Archimedean point from which to take the measure of its object, and communization has no need of a transcendent standpoint of 'withdrawal' or 'secession' from which to launch its 'attack'.

Communist theory does not present an alternative answer to the question of 'what shall we do?', for the abolition of the capitalist class rela-

tion is not something on which one can *decide*. Of course, this question necessarily sometimes faces the concrete individuals and groups who make up the classes of this relation; it would be absurd to claim that it was in itself somehow 'wrong' to pose such a question – the theory of communization as the direct abolition of the capitalist class relation could never invalidate such moments. Individuals and groups move within the dynamics of the class relation and its struggles, intentionally oriented to the world as it presents itself. But sometimes they find themselves in a moment where the fluidity of this movement has broken down, and they have to reflect, to decide upon how best to continue. Tactical thought then obtrudes with its distinctive separations, the symptom of a momentary interruption in the immediate experience of the dynamic. When this emergent tactical thought turns out not to have resolved itself into the overcoming of the problem, and the continuation of involvement in overt struggles presents itself for the time being as an insurmountable problem, this individual or group is thrust into the contemplative standpoint of having a purely external relation to its object, even as it struggles to re-establish a practical link with this object.

In *Call* and *The Coming Insurrection* this basic dilemma assumes a theoretical form. Lapsing back from the highs of a wave of struggles, the tactical question is posed; then as this wave ebbs ever-further – and with it the context which prompted the initial question – theory indicates a completely contemplative standpoint, even as it gesticulates wildly towards action. Its object becomes absolutely external and transcendent while its subject is reduced to fragile, thinly-veiled self-affirmations, and the *'what we must do'* that it presents becomes reduced to a trivial list of survival skills straight out of Ray Mears. In the moment in which *Tiqqun* was born, as the structures of the old workers' movement lay behind it and the field of action became an indeterminate 'globalization' – the horizon of a triumphant liberal capitalism – class belonging appeared as something which had been already cast aside, a mere shed skin, and capital too became correspondingly difficult to identify as the other pole of an inherently antagonistic relation. Here lies the historically-specific content represented by these texts: the indeterminacy of the object of antagonism, the voluntaristic relation to the totality constructed around this antagonism, the indifference to the problem of class and its overcoming. The 'desert' in which *Tiqqun* built its sandcastles was the arid, featureless horizon of a financialized, fin-de-siècle capitalism. Setting out in this desert, unable to grasp it as a passing moment in the dynamic of the class relation, *Tiqqun* could never have anticipated the present crisis, and the struggles that have come with it.

The 'what shall we do?' posed by the end of the wave of struggles which had the anti-globalization movement at its center is now passed; there is little need in the present moment to cast around for practical tips for the re-establishment of some insurrectionary practice, or theoretical justifications for a retreat into 'radical' milieus. It is a cruel historical irony that the French state should find in this standpoint – defined precisely by its helplessness in the face of its object, its fundamental reference to a moment that has passed – the threat of 'terrorism' and an 'ultra-left' worth crushing even further. And that, while it busies itself with the defiant, melancholy outpourings of a stranded insurrectionism, pushing its unhappy protagonists through a high-profile 'terrorist' scandal, tectonic movements are occurring within the global capitalist class relation far more significant, and far more threatening for capitalist society.

The global working class is at present under a very overt attack as the functionaries of capital attempt to stabilise a world system constantly on the brink of disaster, and it has not had any need of insurrectionary pep-talk to 'get started' in its response. The Tiqqunist jargon of authenticity accompanied the outbreak of student occupations in California, but these were of course not the struggles of an insurrectionary 'communization' waged voluntaristically in the desert, against some undefined *they*. These struggles were a specific conjunctural response to the form that the current crisis had taken as it hit the Californian state, and the higher education system in particular. This was a situation which demanded resistance, yet without there being any sense that reformist demands would be at all meaningful – hence the 'no demands' rhetoric of the first wave of these struggles. At the same time, communization of course did not present itself as a direct possibility, and nor was any other ostensibly revolutionary dynamic immediately on the cards. Caught between the necessity of action, the impossibility of reformism, and the lack of any revolutionary horizon whatsoever, these struggles took the form of a transient generalization of occupations and actions for which there could be no clear notion of what it would mean to 'win'. It was the *demandless,* temporary taking of spaces in these struggles that came to be identified with 'communization'. Yet, given the absence of any immediate possibility of actual communization here, the language of yesteryear – 'TAZ', 'autonomy' etc. – would have been more appropriate in characterizing such actions. While such language was, ten years ago, that of the 'radical' wing of movements, in California this flowering of autonomous spaces was the form of the movement itself. Perversely, it was the very anachronism of the Tiqqunist problematic here that enabled it to resonate with a movement that took this form. If Tiqqun's 'communization' is an insurrectionary reinvention of 'TAZ', 'autonomy' etc., formulated at the limit of the historical moment which produced these ideas, in California it met a movement finally adequate to such ideas, but one that was so only as a blocked – yet at the same time necessary – response to the crisis.

It is as a result of this blocked movement that 'communization' has come to be barely differentiable from what people used to call 'autonomy'; just one of the latest terms (alongside 'human strike', 'imaginary party' etc) in the jargon of a basically continuous Anglo-American sensibility. This sensibility always involved a proclivity for abstract, voluntarist self-affirmation – in *Tiqqun* it merely finds itself reflected back at itself – and it should thus be no surprise that here, 'communization' is appropriately abstract, voluntarist, and self-affirming. This arrival of 'communization' at the forefront of radical chic probably means little in itself, but the major movement so far to find its voice in this language is more interesting, for the impasse of this movement is not merely a particular lack of programme or demands, but a symptom of the developing crisis in the class relation. What is coming is not a Tiqqunist insurrection, even if Glenn Beck thinks he spies one in the Arab uprisings. If communization is presenting itself currently, it is in the palpable sense of an impasse in the dynamic of the class relation; this is an era in which the end of this relation looms perceptibly on the horizon, while capital runs into crisis at every turn and the working class is forced to wage a struggle for which there is no plausible victory.

Communization in the Present Tense
Théorie Communiste

In the course of revolutionary struggle, the abolition of the state, of exchange, of the division of labor, of all forms of property, the extension of the situation where everything is freely available as the unification of human activity – in a word, the abolition of classes – are 'measures' that abolish capital, imposed by the very necessities of struggle against the capitalist class. The revolution is communization; it does not have communism as a project and result, but as its very content.

Communization and communism are things of the future, *but it is in the present that we must speak about them.* This is the content of the revolution to come that these struggles signal – in this cycle of struggles – each time that the very fact of acting as a class appears as an external constraint, a limit to overcome. *Within itself, to struggle as a class has become the problem* – it has become its own limit. Hence the struggle of the proletariat as a class signals and produces the revolution as its own supersession, as communization.

a) Crisis, restructuring, cycle of struggle: on the struggle of the proletariat as a class as its own limit

The principal result of the capitalist production process has always been the renewal of the capitalist relation between labor and its conditions: in other words it is a process of self-presupposition.

Until the crisis of the late 1960s, the workers' defeat and the restructuring that followed, there was indeed the self-presupposition of capital, according to the latter's concept, but the contradiction between proletariat and capital was located at this level through the production and confirmation, within this very self-presupposition, of a working class identity through which the cycle of struggles was structured as the competition between two hegemonies, two rival modes of managing and controlling reproduction. This identity was the very substance of the workers' movement.

This workers' identity, whatever the social and political forms of its existence (from the Communist Parties to autonomy; from the Socialist State to the workers' councils), rested entirely on the contradiction which developed in this phase of real subsumption of labor under capital between, on the one hand, the creation and development of labor-power employed by capital in an ever more collective and social way, and on the other, the forms of appropriation by capital of this labor-power in the immediate production process, and in the process of reproduction. This is the conflictual situation which developed in this cycle of struggles as workers' identity – an identity which found its distinguishing features and its immediate modalities of recognition in the 'large factory', in the dichotomy between employment and unemployment, work and training, in the submission of the labor process to the collectivity of workers, in the link between wages, growth and productivity within a national area, in the institutional representations that all this implied, as much in the factory as at the level of the state – i.e. in the delimitation of accumulation within a national area.

The restructuring was the defeat, in the late 1960s and the 1970s, of this entire cycle of struggles founded on workers' identity; the content of the restructuring was the destruction of all that which had become an impediment to the fluidity of the self-presupposition of capital. These impediments consisted, on the one hand, of all the separations, protections and specifications that were erected in opposition to the decline in value of labor-power, insofar as they prevented the working class as a whole, in the continuity of its existence, of its reproduction and expansion, from having to face as such the whole of capital. On the other hand, there were all the constraints of circulation, turnover, and accumulation, which impeded the transformation of the surplus product into surplus-value and additional capital. Any surplus product must be able to find its market anywhere, any surplus-value must be able to find the possibility of operating as additional capital anywhere, i.e. of being transformed into means of production and labor power, without any formalisation of the international cycle (such as the division into blocs, East and West, or into center and periphery) predetermining this transformation. Financial capital was the architect of this restructuring. With the restructuring that was completed in the 1980s, the production of surplus-value and the reproduction of the conditions of this production coincided.

The current cycle of struggles is fundamentally defined by the fact that the contradiction between classes occurs at the level of their respective reproduction, which means that the proletariat finds and confronts its own constitution and existence as a class in its contradiction with capital. From this flows the disappearance of a worker's identity confirmed in the reproduction of capital – i.e. the end of the workers' movement and the concomitant bankruptcy of self-organization and autonomy as a revolutionary perspective. Because the perspective of revolution is no longer a matter of the affirmation of the class, it can no longer be a matter of self-organization. To abolish capital is at the same time to negate oneself as a worker and not to self-organize as such: it's a movement of the abolition of enterprises, of factories, of the product, of exchange (whatever its form).

For the proletariat, to act as a class is currently, on the one hand, to have no other horizon than capital and the categories of its reproduction, and on the other, for the same reason, it is to be in contradiction with and to put into question its own reproduction as a class. This conflict, this *rift* in the action of the proletariat, is the content of class struggle and what is at stake in it. What is now *at stake* in these struggles is that, for the proletariat, to act as a class is the limit of its action as a class – this is now an objective situation of class struggle – and that the limit is constructed as such in the struggles and becomes *class belonging as an external constraint*. This determines the level of conflict with capital, and gives rise to internal conflicts within the struggles themselves. This transformation is a determination of the current contradiction between classes, but it is in every case the particular practice of a struggle at a given moment and in given conditions.

This cycle of struggles is the action of a recomposed working class. It consists, in the core areas of accumulation, in the disappearance of the great workers' bastions and the proletarianization of employees; in the tertiarization of employment (maintenance specialists, equipment operators, truck drivers, shippers, stevedores, etc. – this type of employment now accounts for the majority of workers); in working in smaller companies or sites; in a new division of labor and of the working class with the outsourcing of low value-added processes (involving young workers, often temporary, without career prospects); in the generalization of lean production; in the presence of young workers whose education has broken the continuity of generations succeeding each other and who overwhelmingly reject factory work and the working class condition in general; and in offshoring.

Large concentrations of workers in India and China form part of a global segmentation of the labor force. They can neither be regarded as a renaissance elsewhere of what has disappeared in 'the West' in terms of their global definition, nor in terms of their own inscription in the national context. It was a social system of existence and reproduction that defined working-class identity and was expressed in the workers' movement, and not the mere existence of quantitative material characteristics.[25]

From daily struggles to revolution, there can only be a rupture. But this rupture is signalled in the daily course of the class struggle each time that class belonging appears, within these struggles, as an external constraint which is objectified in capital, in the very course of the proletariat's activity as a class. Currently, the revolution is predicated on the supersession of a contradiction which is constitutive of the class struggle: for the proletariat, being a class is the obstacle that its struggle as a class must get beyond. With the production of class belonging as an external constraint, it is possible to understand *the tipping point of the class struggle* – its supersession – as a produced supersession, on the basis of current struggles. In its struggle against capital, the class turns back against itself, i.e. it treats its own existence, everything that defines it in its relation to capital (and it is nothing but this relation), as the limit of its action. Proletarians do not liberate their 'true individuality', which is denied in capital: revolutionary practice is precisely the coincidence between the change in circumstances and that in human activity or self-transformation.

This is the reason why we can currently speak of communism, and speak of it in the present as a real, existing movement. It is now a fact that revolution is the abolition of all classes, insofar as *action as a class of the proletariat is, for itself, a limit.* This abolition is not a goal that is set, a definition of revolution as a norm to be achieved, but a current content in what the class struggle is itself. To produce class belonging as an external constraint is, for the proletariat, to enter into conflict with its previous situation; this is not 'liberation', nor is it 'autonomy'. This is the 'hardest step to take' in the theoretical understanding and practice of contemporary struggles.

The proletariat does not thereby become a 'purely negative' being. To say that the proletariat only exists as a class in and against capital, that it produces its entire being, its organization, its reality and its constitution as a class in capital and against it, is to say that it is the class of surplus-value producing labor. What has disappeared in the current cycle of struggles, following the restructuring of the 1970s and 1980s, is not this objective existence of the class, but is rather the confirmation of a proletarian identity in the reproduction of capital.

The proletariat can only be revolutionary by recognising itself as a class; it recognizes itself as such in every conflict, and it has to do so all the more in the situation in which its existence as a class is that which it has to confront in the reproduction of capital. We must not be mistaken as to the content of this 'recognition'. For the proletariat to recognize itself as a class will not be its 'return to itself' but rather a total extroversion (a self-externalisation) *as it recognizes itself as a category of the capitalist mode of production*. What we are as a class is immediately nothing other than our relation to capital. For the proletariat, this 'recognition' will in fact consist in a practical cognition, in conflict, not of itself for itself, but of capital – i.e. its de-objectification. The unity of the class can no longer constitute itself on the basis of the wage and demands-based struggle, as a prelude to its revolutionary activity. The unity of the proletariat can only be the activity in which it abolishes itself in abolishing everything that divides it.

From struggles over immediate demands to revolution, there can only be a rupture, a qualitative leap. But this rupture is not a miracle, it is not an alternative; neither is it the simple realisation on the part of the proletariat that there is nothing else to do than revolution in the face of the failure of everything else. 'Revolution is the only solution' is just as inept as talk of the revolutionary dynamic of demands-based struggles. This rupture is produced positively by the unfolding of the cycle of struggles which precedes it; it is *signalled* in the multiplication of *rifts* within the class struggle.

As theorists we are on the look-out for, and we promote, these rifts within the class struggle of the proletariat through which it calls itself into question; in practice, we are actors in them when we are directly involved. We exist in this rupture, in this rift in the proletariat's activity as a class.

There is no longer any perspective for the proletariat on its own basis as class of the capitalist mode of production, other than the capacity to supersede its class existence in the abolition of capital. There is an absolute identity between being in contradiction with capital and being in contradiction with its own situation and definition as a class.

It is through this *rift* within action as a class itself that *communization* becomes a question in the present. This rift within the class struggle, in which the proletariat has no other horizon than capital, and thus simultaneously enters into contradiction with its own action as a class, is the dynamic of this cycle of struggles. Currently the class struggle of the proletariat has identifiable elements or activities which signal its own supersession in its own course.

b) Struggles producing theory [26]

The theory of this cycle of struggle, as it has been presented above, is not an abstract formalization which will then prove that it conforms to reality through examples. It is its practical existence, rather than its intellectual veracity, that it proves in the concrete. It is a particular moment of struggles which themselves are already theoretical (in the sense that they are productive of theory), insofar as they have a critical relation vis-à-vis themselves.

Most often, these are not earthshaking declarations or 'radical' actions but rather all the practices of the proletariat of flight from, or rejection of, its own condition. In current strikes over layoffs, workers often no longer demand to keep their jobs, but increasingly they fight for substantial redundancy payments instead. *Against capital, labor has no future.* It was already strikingly evident in the so-called 'suicidal' struggles of the Cellatex firm in France, where workers threatened to discharge acid into a river and to blow up the factory, threats which were not carried out but which were widely imitated in other conflicts over the closure of firms, that the proletariat is nothing if it is separated from capital and that it bears no future within itself, *from its own nature*, other than the abolition of that by which it exists. It is the de-essentialization of labor which becomes the very activity of the proletariat: both tragically, in its struggles without immediate perspectives (i.e. its suicidal struggles), and as demand for this de-essentialization, as in the struggles of the unemployed and the precarious in the winter of 1998 in France.

Unemployment is no longer clearly separated from employment. The segmentation of the labor force; flexibility; outsourcing; mobility; part-time employment; training; internships and informal work have blurred all the separations.

In the French movement of 1998, and more generally in the struggles of the unemployed in this cycle of struggles, *it was the definition of the unemployed which was upheld as the point of departure for the reformulation of waged employment.* The need for capital to measure everything in labor time and to posit the exploitation of labor as a matter of life or death for it is simultaneously the de-essentialization of living labor relative to the social forces that capital concentrates in itself. This contradiction, inherent in capitalist accumulation, which is a contradiction in capital-in-process, takes the very particular form of the definition of the class vis-à-vis capital; the unemployment of the class claims for itself the status of being the starting-point for such a definition. In the struggles of the unemployed and the precarious, the struggle of the proletariat against capital makes this contradiction its own, and champions it. The same thing occurs when workers who have been sacked don't demand jobs but severance pay instead.

In the same period, the Moulinex employees who had been made redundant set fire to a factory building, thus inscribing themselves in the dynamic of this cycle of struggles, which makes the existence of the proletariat as a class the limit of its class action. Similarly, in 2006, in Savar, 50km north of Dhaka, Bangladesh, two factories were torched and a hundred others ransacked after workers had not been paid for three months. In Algeria, minor wage demands turned into riots, forms of representation were dismissed without new ones being formed, and it was the entirety of the living conditions and reproduction of the proletariat which came into play beyond the demands made by the immediate protagonists of the strike. In China and India, there's no prospect of the formation of a vast *workers' movement* from the proliferation of various types of demands-based action affecting all aspects of life and the reproduction of the working class. These demands-based actions often turn paradoxically on the destruction of the conditions of labor, i.e. of their own raison d'être.

In the case of Argentina, people self-organized as the unemployed of Mosconi, as the workers of Brukman, as slum-residents… but in self-organizing they immediately came up against what they were as an obstacle, which, in the struggle, became that which had to be overcome, and which was seen as such in the practical modalities of these self-organized movements. The proletariat cannot find within itself the capacity to create other inter-individual relations, without overturning and negating what it is itself in this society, i.e. without entering into contradiction with autonomy and its dynamic. Self-organization is perhaps the first act of revolution, but all the following acts are directed against it (i.e. against self-organization). In Argentina it was the determinations of the proletariat as a class of this society (i.e. property, exchange, the division of labor, the relation between men and women ...) which were effectively undermined by the way productive activities were undertaken, i.e. in the actual modalities of their realisation. It is thus that the revolution as communization becomes credible.

In France in November 2005, in the *banlieues*, the rioters didn't demand anything, they attacked their own condition, they made everything that produces and defines them their target. Rioters revealed and attacked *the proletarian situation now*: the worldwide precarization of the labor force. In doing so they immediately made obsolete, in the very moment in which such a demand could have been articulated, any desire to be an 'ordinary proletarian'.

Three months later, in spring 2006, still in France, as a demands-based movement, the student movement against the CPE could only comprehend itself by becoming the general movement of the precarious; but in doing so it would either negate its own specificity, or it would inevitably be forced to collide more or less violently with all those who had shown in the riots of November 2005 that the demand to be an 'ordinary proletarian' was obsolete. To achieve the demand through its expansion would in effect be to sabotage it. What credibility was there in a link-up with the November rioters on the basis of a stable job for all? On the one hand, this link-up was objectively inscribed in the genetic code of the movement; on the other hand, the very necessity of this link-up induced an internal love-hate dynamic, just as objective, within the movement. *The struggle against the CPE was a movement of demands, the satisfaction of which would have been unacceptable to itself as a movement of demands.*

In the Greek riots, the proletariat didn't demand anything, and didn't consider itself to be opposed to capital as the foundation of any alternative. But if these riots were a movement of the class, they didn't constitute a struggle in what is the very matrix of classes: *production*. It is in this way that these riots were able to make the key achievement of producing and targeting class belonging as a constraint, but they could only reach this point by confronting this *glass floor* of production as their limit. And the ways in which this movement produced this external constraint (the aims, the unfolding of the riots, the composition of the rioters…) was intrinsically defined by this limit: the relation of exploitation as coercion pure and simple. Attacking institutions and the forms of social reproduction, taken in themselves, was on the one hand what constituted the movement, and what constituted its force, but this was also the expression of its limits.

Students without a future, young immigrants, precarious workers, these are all proletarians who every day live the reproduction of capitalist social relations as coercion; coercion is *included* in this reproduction because they are proletarians, but they experience it every day as *separated* and aleatory (accidental and non-necessary) in relation to production itself. At the same time as they struggle in this moment of coercion which they experience as separated, they only conceive of and live this separation as a lack in their own struggle against this mode of production.

It is in this way that this movement produced class belonging as an exterior constraint, but only in this way. It is in this way that it locates itself at the level of this cycle of struggles and is one of its determining historical moments.

In their own practice and in their struggle, proletarians called themselves into question as proletarians, but only by autonomizing the moments and the instances of social reproduction in their attacks and their aims. Reproduction and production of capital remained foreign to each other.

In Guadeloupe, the importance of unemployment, and of the part of the population that lives from benefits and or from an underground economy, means that wage-demands are a contradiction in terms. This contradiction structured the course of events between, on the one hand, the LKP, which was centered on permanent workers (essentially in public services) but which attempted to hold the terms of this contradiction together through the multiplication and the infinite diversity of demands, and, on the other, the absurdity of central wage-demands for the majority of people on the barricades, in the looting, and in the attacks on public buildings. The demand was destabilized in the very course of the struggle; it was contested, as was its form of organization, but the specific forms of exploitation of the entire population, inherited from its colonial history, were able to prevent this contradiction from breaking out more violently at the heart of the movement (it is important to note that the only death was that of a trade-unionist killed on a barricade). From this point of view, the production of class belonging as an external constraint was more a sociological state, more a sort of schizophrenia, than something at stake in the struggle.

In general, with the outbreak of the current crisis, the wage demand is currently characterized by a dynamic that wasn't previously possible. It is an *internal* dynamic which comes about as a result of the *whole* relation between proletariat and capital in the capitalist mode of production such as it emerged from the restructuring and such as it is now entering into crisis. The wage demand has changed its meaning.

In the succession of financial crises which for the last twenty years or so have regulated the current mode of valorization of capital, the subprime crisis is the first to have taken as its point of departure not the financial assets that refer to capital investments, but household consumption, and more precisely that of the poorest households. In this respect it inaugurates a specific crisis of the wage relation of restructured capitalism, in which the continual decrease in the share of wages in the wealth produced, both in the core countries and in the emerging ones, remains definitive.

The 'distribution of wealth', from being essentially conflictual in the capitalist mode of production, has become *taboo*, as was confirmed in the recent movement of strikes and blockades (October-November 2010) following the reform of the pensions system in France. In restructured capitalism (the beginnings of the crisis of which we are currently experiencing), the reproduction of labor power was subjected to a *double decoupling*. On the one hand a decoupling between the valorization of capital and the reproduction of labor power and, on the other, a decoupling between consumption and the wage as income.

Of course, the division of the working day into necessary and surplus labor has always been definitive of the class struggle. But now, in the struggle over this division, it is paradoxically in the proletariat's definition to the very depth of its being as a class of this mode of production, *and as nothing else*, that it is apparent in practice, and in a conflictual way, that its existence as a class is the limit of its own struggle as a class. This is *currently* the central character of the wage demand in class struggle. In the most trivial course of the wage demand, the proletariat sees its own existence as a class objectify itself as something which is alien to it to the extent that the capitalist relation itself places *it in its heart* as something *alien*.

The current crisis broke out because proletarians could no longer repay their loans. It broke out on the very basis of the wage relation which gave rise to the financialization of the capitalist economy: wage cuts as a requirement for 'value creation' and global competition within the labor force. It was this functional necessity that returned, but in a negative fashion, within the historical mode of capital accumulation with the detonation of the subprime crisis. It is now the wage relation that is at the core of the current crisis.[27] The current crisis is the beginning of the phase of reversal of the determinations and dynamic of capitalism as it had emerged from the restructuring of the 1970s and 1980s.

c) Two or three things we know about it

It is because the proletariat is not-capital, because it is the dissolution of all existing conditions (labor, exchange, division of labor, property), that it finds here the content of its *revolutionary action* as *communist measures*: the abolition of property, of the division of labor, of exchange and of value. Class belonging as external constraint is thus *in itself* a content, that is to say a practice, which supersedes itself in communizing measures when the limit of the struggle as a class is manifested. *Communization* is nothing other than *communist measures* taken as simple *measures of struggle* by the proletariat against capital.

It is the paucity of surplus-value relative to accumulated capital which is at the heart of the crisis of exploitation: if, at the heart of the *contradiction* between the proletariat and capital there was not the question of labor which is productive of *surplus-value*; if there was only a problem of distribution, i.e. if the contradiction between the proletariat and capital wasn't a contradiction for the very thing, namely the capitalist mode of production, whose dynamic it constitutes; i.e. if it was not a 'game which produces the abolition of its own rule', the revolution would remain a pious wish. Hatred of capital and the desire for another life are only the necessary ideological expressions of this contradiction for-itself which is exploitation.

It is not through an attack on the side of the nature of labor as productive of surplus-value that the demands-based struggle is superseded (which would always devolve back to a problem of distribution), but through an attack on the side of the means of production as capital. The attack against the capitalist nature of the means of production is their abolition as value absorbing labor in order to valorize itself; it is the extension of the situation where everything is freely available, the destruction (perhaps physical) of certain means of production, their abolition as the factories in which it is defined what it is to be a product, i.e. the matrices of exchange and commerce; it is their definition, their absorption in individual, intersubjective relations; it is the abolition of the division of labor such as it is inscribed in urban zoning, in the material configuration of buildings, in the separation between town and country, in the very existence of something which is called a factory or a point of production. Relations between individuals are fixed in things, because exchange value is by nature material.[28] The abolition of value is a concrete transformation of the landscape in which we live, it is a new geography. The abolition of social relations is a very material affair.

In communism, appropriation no longer has any currency, because it is the very notion of the 'product' which is abolished. Of course, there are objects which are used to produce, others which are directly consumed, and others still which are used for both. But to speak of 'products' and to pose the question of their circulation, their distribution or their 'transfer', i.e. to conceive a moment of appropriation, is to presuppose points of rupture, of 'coagulation' of human activity: the market in market societies, the depot where goods are freely available in certain visions of communism. The 'product' is not a simple thing. To speak of the 'product' is to suppose that a result of human activity appears as *finite* vis-à-vis another such result or the sphere of other such results. It is not from the 'product' that we must proceed, but from activity.

In communism, human activity is infinite because it is indivisible. It has concrete or abstract results, but these results are never 'products', for that would raise the question of their appropriation or of their transfer under some given mode. If we can speak of *infinite human activity* in communism, it is because the capitalist mode of production already allows us to see – albeit contradictorily and not as a 'good side' – human activity as a continuous global social flux, and the *'general intellect'* or the 'collective worker' as the dominant force of production. The social character of production does not prefigure anything: it merely renders the basis of value contradictory.

The destruction of exchange means the workers attacking the banks which hold their accounts and those of other workers, thus making it necessary to do without; it means the workers communicating their 'products' to themselves and the community directly and without a market, thereby abolishing themselves as workers; it means the obligation for the whole class to organize itself to seek food in the sectors to be communized, etc. There is no measure which, in itself, taken separately, is 'communism'. What is communist is not 'violence' in itself, nor 'distribution' of the shit that we inherit from class society, nor 'collectivization' of surplus-value sucking machines: it is the nature of the movement which connects these actions, underlies them, renders them the moments of a process which can only communize ever further, or be crushed.

A revolution cannot be carried out without taking communist

measures: dissolving wage labor; communizing supplies, clothing, housing; seizing all the weapons (the destructive ones, but also telecommunications, food, etc.); integrating the destitute (including those of us who will have reduced ourselves to this state), the unemployed, ruined farmers, rootless drop-out students.

From the moment in which we begin to consume freely, it is necessary to reproduce that which is consumed; it is thus necessary to seize the means of transport, of telecommunications, and enter into contact with other sectors; so doing, we will run up against the opposition of armed groups. The confrontation with the state immediately poses the problem of arms, which can only be solved by setting up a distribution network to support combat in an almost infinite multiplicity of places. Military and social activities are inseparable, simultaneous, and mutually interpenetrating: the constitution of a front or of determinate zones of combat is the death of the revolution. From the moment in which proletarians dismantle the laws of commodity relations, there is no turning back. The deepening and extension of this social process gives flesh and blood to new relations, and enables the integration of more and more non-proletarians to the communizing class which is simultaneously in the process of constituting and dissolving itself. It permits the abolition to an ever greater extent of all competition and division between proletarians, making this the content and the unfolding of its armed confrontation with those whom the capitalist class can still mobilize, integrate and reproduce within its social relations.

This is why all the measures of communization will have to be a vigorous action for the dismantling of the connections which link our enemies and their material support: these will have to be rapidly destroyed, without the possibility of return. Communization is not the peaceful organization of the situation where everything is freely available and of a pleasant way of life amongst proletarians. The dictatorship of the social movement of communization is the process of the integration of humanity into the proletariat which is in the process of disappearing. The strict delimitation of the proletariat in comparison with other classes and its struggle against all commodity production are at the same time a process which *constrains* the strata of the salaried *petite-bourgeoisie*, the class of social (middle-) management, to join the communizing class. Proletarians 'are' not revolutionaries like the sky 'is' blue, merely because they 'are' waged and exploited, or even because they are the dissolution of existing conditions. In their self-transformation, *which has as its point of departure what they are*, they constitute themselves as a revolutionary class. The movement in which the proletariat is defined in practice as the movement of the constitution of the human community is the reality of the abolition of classes. The social movement in Argentina was confronted by, and posed, the question of the relations between proletarians in employment, the unemployed, and the excluded and middle strata. It only provided extremely fragmentary responses, of which the most interesting is without doubt that of its territorial organization. The revolution, which in this cycle of struggles can no longer be anything but communization, supersedes the dilemma between the Leninist or democratic class alliances and Gorter's 'proletariat alone': two different types of defeat.

The only way of overcoming the conflicts between the unemployed and those with jobs, between the skilled and the unskilled, is to carry out measures of communization which remove the very basis of this division, right from the start and in the course of the armed struggle. This is something which the occupied factories in Argentina, when confronted by this question, tried only very marginally, being generally satisfied (cf. Zanon) with some charitable redistribution to groups of *piqueteros*. In the absence of this, capital will play on this fragmentation throughout the movement, and will find its Noske and Scheidemann amongst the self-organized.

In fact, as already shown by the German revolution, it is a question of dissolving the middle strata by taking concrete communist measures which compel them to begin to join the proletariat, i.e. to achieve their 'proletarianization'. Nowadays, in developed countries, the question is at the same time simpler and more dangerous. On the one hand a massive majority of the middle strata is salaried and thus no longer has a material base to its social position; its role of management and direction of capitalist cooperation is essential but ever rendered precarious; its social position depends upon the very fragile mechanism of the subtraction of fractions of surplus value. On the other hand, however, and for these very same reasons, its formal proximity to the proletariat pushes it to present, in these struggles, national or democratic alternative managerial 'solutions' which would preserve its own positions.

The essential question which we will have to solve is to understand how we extend communism, before it is suffocated in the pincers of the commodity; how we integrate agriculture so as not to have to exchange with farmers; how we do away with the exchange-based relations of our adversary to impose on him the logic of the communization of relations and of the seizure of goods; how we dissolve the block of fear through the revolution.

To conclude, capital is not abolished for communism but through communism, more precisely through its production. Indeed, communist measures must be distinguished from communism: they are not embryos of communism, but rather they are its production. This is not a period of transition, it is the revolution: communization is only the *communist production of communism*. The struggle against capital is what differentiates communist measures from communism. The revolutionary activity of the proletariat always has as its content the mediation of the abolition of capital through its relation to capital: this is neither one branch of an alternative in competition with another, nor communism as immediatism.

(translation: Endnotes.)

The need for communism traverses the entirety of the society of capital. The merit of *Call* lies in taking note of this, and of trying to design strategies which live up to this realization.[30] Its weakness comes from the continually resurgent temptation to think that the desire to establish different relations suffices to start producing them.

Primo

Call, as its name indicates, is not a text of analysis or debate. Its purpose is not to convince or denounce, it is to affirm, to expose, and on this basis to announce a strategy for revolution. Must we therefore conclude, with Gilles Dauvé, that 'a call cannot be refuted, either we hear it or we pay it no heed'?[31]

Call itself, in its refusal to discuss the 'sensibly [self-]evident' (p.21) encourages this reaction from the first lines of the first *scholium:* 'This is a call. That is to say it aims at those who can hear it. The question is not to demonstrate, to argue, to convince. We will go straight to the *evident.*' (p.4) But, at the same time, *Call* is the typical product of a debate inherent to the very existence of the 'area which poses the question of communization': and pursuing this debate to its conclusion is a preliminary to any emergence of a self-conscious 'communizing movement' within this area.[32]

It is to be understood that the objective of these reflections is not to make a textual commentary on *Call,* to be exhaustive, or to interpret the thought or intentions of the authors in an academic manner. Even if it is one of its expressions, *Call* is far from posing an unanimity in the struggles which, in one form or another, pose the question of communization: it was on the contrary the occasion for numerous discussions. As *Call* illustrates quite well a certain proclivity into which the whole 'area which poses the question of communization', on the basis of its very problematic, is capable of falling, to put in writing these critiques is an occasion to nourish the debate.

Secundo

That which characterizes the communizing current is not so much a common interpretation of communism as an attention paid to the process of its production, that is, what we term communization. *Call* explicitly situates itself in this perspective: 'As we apprehend it, the process of instituting communism can only take the form of a collection of *acts of communization* ... Insurrection itself is just an accelerator, a decisive moment in this process' (p.66). But contrary to *Meeting,* whose problematic is to interrogate the concept of communication, *Call* gives communization a determinate content...

In *Call* the term communization is systematically understood as 'making common'. In the previous quotation for instance the 'acts of communization' are described as 'making common such-and-such space, such-and-such machine, such-and-such knowledge'. That which is put in common is *use*, as when it is said that to communize a space is to liberate its use. This sense is even more visible in other parts of the text. For example:

> In Europe, the integration of workers' organizations into the state management apparatus – the foundation of social democracy – was paid for with the renunciation of all ability to be a nuisance. Here too the emergence of the labor movement was a matter of material solidarities, of an urgent need for communism. The *Maisons du Peuple* were the last shelters for this indistinction between the need for immediate communization and the strategic requirements of a practical implementation of the revolutionary process. (p.54)

Even if communization is conceived as the communization of relations it is first of all on the basis of a common usage: 'Communizing a place means: setting its use free, and on the basis of this liberation experimenting with refined, intensified, and complexified relations.' (p.68)

In the same logic, if communization is 'making common', then communism is systematically assimilated with 'sharing'. The theme of sharing is omnipresent in *Call*. One finds is particularly developed in the *scholium* to Proposition V in the following terms:

> That in us which is most singular calls to be shared. But we note this: not only is that which we have to share obviously incompatible with the prevailing order, but this order strives to track down any form of sharing of which it does not lay down the rules. (p.50)

Sharing is the basis of collective action as envisaged by *Call*: 'We say that squatting will only make sense again for us provided that we clarify the basis of the sharing we enter into.' (p.52)

Tertio

The point is not that 'sharing' and communism have nothing to do with another, but we have trouble understanding how they can be synonymous. Sharing already exists in capitalism: social institutions as important as the family function on the basis of sharing, and even in the countries where capitalism is the oldest and where the familial relation reduces itself to its simplest expression (the parent/child relation), capital, even economically, would not survive without this form of social sharing.

Call recognizes, in a negative sense, that sharing is also constitutive of the capitalist order in affirming that 'the dominant order ... strives to track down any form of sharing of which it does not lay down the rules.' But then are we to understand that any sharing not controlled by the 'dominant order' is a communist sharing? We can imagine so given that communism is purely and simply assimilated to sharing minus control: 'the question of communism is, on one hand, to do away with the police, and on the other, to elaborate modes of sharing, uses, between those who live together.' (p.64)

It is true that the point is still to 'elaborate modes of sharing'. We also find further along: 'It belongs to the communist way that we explain to ourselves and formulate the basis of our sharing.' (p.66) Thus communist sharing is not given, it is to be elaborated. But how? Here the text eats its tail. A certain mode of sharing leads to communism, OK, but which? Response, in substance: the one that leads to communism... Nothing more is said on what can differentiate it from the sharing admitted in the world of capital other than the fact that this particular sharing must lead to a redefinition of relations:

> So communism starts from the experience of sharing. And first, from the sharing of our needs. Needs are not what capitalist rule has accustomed us to. *To need is never about needing things without*

at the same time needing worlds. (pp.64-5)

From then on the definitions of communism multiply: 'By communism we mean *a certain discipline of the attention.*' (p.65) Or again: 'The communist question is about the elaboration of our relationship to the world, to beings, to ourselves.' (p.63)

Among all these definitions there is one which shines out by its absence: communism as the suppression of class society. Certainly *Call* affirms that 'Communism does not consist in the elaboration *of new relations of production, but indeed in the abolition of those relations.*' (p.68) However, it is never a question of the 'abolition of class relations' – nonetheless a classical corollary of the 'abolition of relations of production'.

The term 'class struggle' and 'proletariat' are never employed. As for the adjective 'worker', it serves only to qualify the old 'movement', something which at one time incarnated the communist aspiration but no longer... *Call,* that is, doesn't affirm that the division of society into antagonistic social classes doesn't exist, or existed once but is now as surpassed as the usage of steam on the railway. It simply doesn't speak of it. Capitalism is certainly present in the text, but far from being seen as the system which englobes the totality of social reality, it is described essentially through its mechanisms of control, to the point where we could as well call it 'empire' as call it 'capitalism', or call it 'civilization':

> There is a general context – capitalism, civilization, empire, call it what you wish – that not only intends to control each situation but, even worse, tries to make sure that there is, as often as possible, *no situation.* The streets and the houses, the language and the affects, and the worldwide tempo that sets the pace of it all, have been adjusted *for that purpose only.* (p.9)

It is precisely because capitalism is considered as an assemblage and not as a system that *Call* supposes that there exists a possible 'beyond' to the world of capital.

Quarto

Let us return for a moment to the quotation from the *scholium* of Proposition VI: 'communism does not consist in the elaboration *of new relations of production, but indeed in the abolition of those relations.*' (p.68) The text which follows contains a surprising affirmation: these 'relations of production' can be abolished immediately 'between ourselves':

> Not having relations of production with our world or between ourselves means never letting the search for results become more important than the attention to the process; casting from ourselves all forms of valorization; making sure we do not disconnect affection and cooperation (p.68).

The problem is that a 'relation of production' is not a particular relation between two people, or even a hundred, or a thousand. It is a generalized social relation which cannot be abolished locally because even where people would not 'live' relations of production between themselves, they would no less be incorporated in relations of production which structure capitalist society as a whole.

A 'relation of production' is not a relation between individuals, or at least it cannot be only that: two people do not maintain between themselves a private relation of production which they could somehow negate by their sole common volition. One might object that *Call* would also not see relations of production as inter-individual relations, simply because its philosophy banishes the concept of the individual. And in the text of *Call*, 'forms of life' and other 'relations to the world' do indeed traverse bodies. But 'relations of production' are no more relations between forms of life or worlds than they are relations between persons. The entities which are linked by 'relations of production' are just those which the same relations define: it is the position in the relation of production which determines the entities, and not the contrary. Relations of production are relations between classes.

It is certain that the division of society into classes would be infinitely more visible if inter-individual relations were the brute and unreserved translation of relations of production. The proletarian would doff his cap in passing to the capitalist with his top hat and cigar, and there would be nothing more to say. But unfortunately thing are a little more complicated, and 'existential liberalism' is not the unique translation of the effect of relations of production in everyday life...

Call is not mistaken when it says: 'capitalism has revealed itself to be not merely a mode of production, but a reduction of all relations, in the last instance, to relations of production.' (p.67) But this 'reduction in the last instance' is not a collapsing. There is obviously a link, tenuous and complex but nonetheless palpable, between, on the one hand, the sociability at the office, the posture of bodies in the large metropoles, or indeed what *Call* designates as 'existential liberalism', and, on the other hand, the 'relations of production'. But it is a link, not an identity.

'Marxism' would say that 'the relations of production *determine* the relations that we can maintain among ourselves': but 'determine' implies a necessity of the very form of the link just where we can observe an extreme diversity. We could also say that 'the relations of production *contain* the relations that we can maintain among ourselves'. They model and restrain them without exhausting them. We have both a certain margin of maneuver (it's on this that *Call* counts) and an equally certain limit (it's this which *Call* doesn't see).

Communization and its Discontents

Quito

Any workers' cooperative can abolish 'relations of production' between its members in the sense understood by *Call*. Would it thereby free itself from capitalist valorization? Financial circuits, commercialization, productivity standards... everything is there so that the workers of the cooperative self-exploit as surely as if the boss was still physically looming over them. Similarly, would a community whose members worked in common and didn't engage in monetary relations among themselves thereby escape 'relations of production'? On the condition of transforming communism into a series of principles to be respected we might perhaps be able to maintain the illusion for a while. But this would be to forget that every point of contact between the community and its exterior would be the occasion to see the 'relations of production' reassert their rights and reintroduce the whole community into class relations: juridical statutes of occupied buildings and land, the supply of provisions, energy, the sale of the surplus...

Sexto

Call is an 'alternative'[33] text because the existence of communism is considered as possible at a moment when capitalism still reigns.

Sure, it's not seen as communism in its final state, for the latter must first constitute itself as a force and 'deepen' itself as a preliminary to revolution; and its only after the insurrection, the moment of acceleration of the process, that communism establishes itself as the universal social relation.

Nonetheless the sense of the text is clear: even in the form of fragments, of instants to explore and reproduce, of 'grace' to research, moments of communism are already to be had. The point is only to recognize them, and on that basis, to organize.

Septimo

I don't agree with Dauvé, for whom *Call* is exempt from all trace of the alternative because

> communization is defined as antagonistic to this world. In irreconcilable and violent conflict with it (to the point of illegality). It differs therefore from the alternative which searches (and often succeeds) in making itself accepted at the margin, and in durably coexisting with the state and wage labor.[34]

Pacifism plays no part in the necessary definition of the alternative: those who one could call the 'confrontational alternatives' are far from being marginal in this type of movement.

To take an example which has nothing to do with *Call*, but which is significant because it is caricatural, one could recall that in the *No Border* camp of Strasbourg 2002 this tendency was present to a very large degree. This camp organized against the Shengen information system (SIS), drew together between one and two thousand people and was the occasion for, *at the same time*, an ephemeral 'self-organized' village lived by certain members as a veritable Temporary Autonomous Zone (with the all the folklore one can imagine) and a week of disruptive actions in the city of Strasbourg. Certainly the actions and demonstrations weren't characterized by an extreme violence,[35] but they were in any case all explicitly anti-legalist and sought to defy the state on its terrain. There were no doubt tensions between a more 'activist' tendency and those who wanted above all to defend the marvelous experience of this self-managed camp, but many people pursued these two objectives whilst seeing them as perfectly complementary.

Being 'alternative' consists in the belief that we can, with limited numbers of people, establish relations within the world of capital which would be already a prefiguration of communism (even if one doesn't use this term). The inverse position holds that, as long capital as a social relation is not abolished, nothing which can resemble communism can be lived.

Thus those who often designate themselves as alternative imagine therefore that, in places like the No Border camp at Strasbourg, or in the Vaag camp which followed it, in squats, or wherever else, moments can be lived which approximate a society liberated from capital, from money, and 'domination'. And that all this can come from an effort of individuals to free themselves from bad 'ideas' that society has inculcated in them. For example, ceasing to be sexist or patriarchal through a series of measures which address behavior, language, etc.

Certain of these alternatives are pacifist. Others think that their desires are not compatible with the maintenance of the society of capital and are perfectly ready for illegal or violent struggle.

One also finds those who think that *only the struggle* offers today the possibility of living moments of communism: the alternative is for them indissociable from anti-capitalist activism. The latter will often shrink from the appellation 'alternative' precisely because they fear being assimilated to pacifism. It's in the last category that one could range those who write: 'No experience of communism at the present time can survive without getting organized, tying itself to others, putting itself in crisis, waging war.' (p.65)

At the other extreme a rigorously anti-alternative position can be found, for example, in *Théorie Communiste* (TC), whose concept of the 'self-transformation of proletarians' draws attention to the hiatus which can exist between what can be lived in the society of capital and what will be lived after the moment that communism will have been produced. This leads the members of TC, and those who adhere to their theses, to see in every practical attempt to pose the communist question a demonstration of the inevitably 'alternative' character of every maneuver of this type.

There is also the position that I have developed in 'Three Theses on Communization'.[36] The point is to take account of the essential critique addressed to the 'alternative' (no possibility of developing communism within the world of capital); but to recognize that there is also necessarily a relation between that which proletarians are today and that which will one day allow them to produce communism, in other words, that it is possible to practically address problematics related to communism, even if it's impossible today to live something which 'tends towards' communism or prefigures it. I've thus argued that the communizing movement is characterized by the fact that it already poses in struggles questions which have the same nature as those which will lead to the production of communism at the moment of the revolution; but that the responses that it brings, cobbled together with what capital renders possible today, are not themselves communist.

Octavo

We do find in *Call* an explicit critique of the 'alternative':

> By dint of seeing the enemy as a subject that faces us – instead of *feeling* it as a relationship that *holds us* – we confine ourselves to the struggle against confinement. We reproduce under the pretext of an 'alternative' the worst kind of dominant relationships. We start selling as a commodity the very struggle against the commodity. Hence we get the authorities of the anti-authoritarian struggle, chauvinist feminism, and anti-fascist lynchings. (pp.8-9)

Or again:

> And then there is this mystification: that caught in the course of a world that displeases us, there would be proposals to make, alternatives to find. That we could, in other words, lift ourselves out of the situation that we are in, to discuss it in a calm way, between

reasonable people. But no, there is nothing beyond the situation. There is no outside to the world civil war. We are irremediably *there*. (p.74)

It must be said that the second critique is more addressed to the pacifist alternative than to the alternative *tout court*. Yet the question is still to understand why *Call*, whilst posing a critique of the alternative, nonetheless leans irresistibly towards it?

The response can be perhaps found in Proposition VI: 'In a general way, we do not see how anything else but a force, a reality able to survive the total dislocation of capitalism, could truly attack it, could pursue the offensive until the very moment of dislocation' (p.70). All the difficulty of revolutionary theory can be found hidden beneath this phrase: the point is to understand the overthrowing of capitalism as a process that is not itself capitalist – since in the end it has the capacity to destroy capitalism – and yet is nonetheless born within the capitalist social relation.

It's in this sense that *Call* is representative of a debate which traverses the area which poses the question of communization. As its practice is manifestly not communist, and cannot be, this area has the temptation to locate the unique reason for the nonexistence of responses to the communising questions that it poses in the weakness of its force or activity.

Nono

We can easily understand that the Party that *Call* speaks of has nothing to do with an avant-garde. In effect, whilst the Leninist party prepares the revolution, or more precisely the coup d'état, the party in question in *Call* directly produces communism, at least the communism of the pre-revolutionary period. Even more: it *is* this communism: 'The practice of communism, as we live it, we call "the Party." When we overcome an obstacle together or when we reach a higher level of sharing, we say that "we are building the Party."' (p.65) The Party is not the avant-garde, it is the whole camp. It englobes even those who have not yet had any association: 'Certainly others, who we do not know yet, are building the Party elsewhere. This call is addressed to them.' (p.65)

The ticks of language the most revealing of the alternative temptation which progressively bares itself out in *Call* are systematically associated with the evocation of the party:

> Looking closer at it, the Party could be nothing but this: the formation of sensibility as a force. The deployment of an archipelago of worlds. What would a political force, under empire, be that didn't have its farms, its schools, its arms, its medicines, its collective houses, its editing desks, its printers, its covered trucks and its bridgeheads in the metropole? It seems more and more absurd that some of us still have to work for capital – aside from the necessary tasks of infiltration. (pp.66-7)

But can one really believe that if we are no longer employed by this or that firm or government we cease to 'work for capital'? And that one has thereby effected a 'secession ... with the process of capitalist valorization' (p.10)? That which distinguishes real subsumption, that is, this period in which capital has in a certain manner absorbed the totality of social reality rather than remaining restricted to the productive process, is that *any activity* is capable of becoming a part of the process of valorization.

Decimo

Call ends, in strategic terms, at an impasse. It is recognized in the last paragraph, which concludes the work with a 'bet', that is to say something not susceptible to argument:

> We will be told: you are caught in an alternative which will condemn you in one way or another: either you manage to constitute a threat to empire, in which case you will be quickly eliminated; or you will not manage to constitute such a threat, and you will have once again destroyed yourselves. There remains only the wager on the existence of another term, a thin ridge, just enough for us to walk on. Just enough for *all those who can hear* to walk and live. (p.88)

How is the material force in formation, the party, to concretely escape repression? Where are 'its farms, its schools, its arms, its medicines, its collective houses, its editing desks, its printers, its covered trucks and its bridgeheads in the metropole' going to hide? Such activities have no need to be subversive to be repressed. In the end, everything is illegal: without even speaking of arms, it is forbidden to practice medicine, to work, to drive, without the corresponding diplomas, contracts or licenses. Even the LETS, the local exchange systems, were once in the firing line of the financial regulators.

All the alternative communities which have existed for a certain time resolved the question in the same way, and in fact there are only two. An experience such as that can only subsist as long as it respects the legality of capital. There is nothing to stop those who have the means creating hospitals, schools, or private collective farms. But on what possible basis can we say they are 'communizing'?

The condition of the confrontation with the legality of capital is to not become attached to a place, a structure, or a durable movement, which would signify defeat. *Call* accords, with reason, much importance to spaces: 'For this, we need places. Places to get organized, to share and develop the required techniques. To learn to handle all that may prove necessary. To co-operate.' (p.57). The space as a point of assembly in the struggle is a mode of organization which has proven itself. But inherent to such spaces is the need to ceaselessly efface themselves before the repression that they attract:

when they eternalize themselves it is simply the sign that they have ceased to be active.

Uno décimo

One of the regrettable consequences of the manner in which *Call* envisages, under capitalism, the growth of a communist camp which reinforces and deepens itself through self-organization is that the way thus traced becomes exclusive of all others. Communism, rather than being produced collectively and universally by the proletariat destroying capital in forms that we cannot determine in advance, is predefined by the configurations that one can give it today, in the very heart of the world of capital.

Yet, the conception that we can have today of communism is itself to be historicized, it is implicated in a stage of development of capitalism. It is this kind of thing that *Call* misses completely. As messianic as the conceptions of communism in *Call* might be, they will always remain the product of present times: and they invariably lack the possible richness of definitions of communism as a universal social relation.

Yet this communism as universal social relation, if it exists one day, will be produced in circumstances (the general crisis of social relations, insurrection, the total destruction of capitalism) whose actual development remains for the most part unknown to us. What will be the communizing measures, those which will allow the concrete production of communism? One can certainly have an opinion on this question; but how can we say whether this opinion can grasp at present what communization will or will not be. Even reflection on the most interesting historical examples on this subject – Spain in the '30s, Italy in the '70s – will never permit us to predict the future to that degree.

In calling for the constitution of a communist camp on the basis of what it defines in the present as communism, *Call* freezes its vision of communism. According to its logic, only those communizing forces capable of self-organizing under capital will be capable of carrying out an insurrection tomorrow; and those forms that are capable of self-organization in the Party are alone communist. How is the Party, supposing that it is formed along the lines delineated in *Call*, to judge the chaotic evolutions of future class struggles? It will only judge them communist insofar as they join it, since it will itself be communism.

The Party will miss everything that will develop in the forms, moments, and circumstances that it will not have been able to foresee; and it will act as their censor. Already the tone of *Call*, often very severe, suggests a separation between 'good' communists, those who've known how to perform 'secession', and 'bad' proletarians who've done nothing other than submit to capital. As if all those who haven't already seceded will never be able to intervene in communization. Moreover, *Call* affirms that all those who want communism must cease to work for capital. How can we imagine that we can create communism while proposing a revolutionary strategy of which the first measure is rupture with all those who 'work for capital'? Especially since a good reason to one day produce communism would perhaps be precisely to have, until then, 'worked for capital'.

Duo decimo

Call falls into a common trap for those who try to pose the question of communization in an at least somewhat practical manner: the responses that we try to bring forward today seem to define a space which only veritable insurgents could populate, whilst the others, those who remain apart from this insurgency, remain nothing but proletarians integrated to capital.

A journal published in Toulouse is quite representative of this manner of thinking. Entitled *WE [NOUS]*, this zine presents on the cover of its 7th issue a drawing of a person walking on a tightrope over a canyon which separates *US [NOUS]* from the world of capital, represented by factories, nuclear power plants, houses, bosses, cops, but also powerless workers and anesthetized television viewers.

In this regard the manner in which *Call* employs the first person plural is not totally innocent.[37] Certainly *Call* takes care to not oppose *US* and *THEM*, but paraphrasing Heidegger, *NOUS* and *ON*.[38] The WE [*NOUS*] of *Call* (like that of Toulouse) is open: 'The "we" [*NOUS*] that speaks here is not a delimitable, isolated we, the we of a group. It is the we *of a position*' (p.10). But this position is the one that affirms on the back-cover that 'WE HAVE BEGUN'. Those who have begun have already advanced on the road to revolution. It is made explicit in the following formula: 'The overthrowing of capitalism will come from those who are able to create the conditions for other types of relations' (p.67). *Call* imagines, as a road to communism, only that which its authors have chosen to follow: here is the sense of a 'WE' which is finally less a position than a trajectory. In effect certain of those who find themselves in 'the area that poses the question of communization' have been able to live a form of 'secession': but such a rupture inscribes itself in a logic of an epoch where communization is a marginal question. One can happily think that a generalized crisis of social relations will introduce many other modes of adhesion to the communist idea. The revolution will not simply be the act of squatters or ex-squatters! To think the contrary is to believe that revolution will only come about on the condition that revolutionary subjectivity has won over the masses, yet the revolution will be at the same time the moment of disobjectification of the capitalist social relation and that of the desubjectification of the question of communization.

Terco decimo

We avoid the foregoing trap if we recognize that, in our epoch, all the responses that can be found to the question of communization are the responses of our epoch: that is to say destined to become obsolete from the moment that the situation will be sufficiently modified so that an until then minority question is in everyone's mouth. The communizing problematic, just like the conception that we can have of communism, is itself historic. If the point of continuity between current struggles and the revolution is indeed the question of communization, this question, already diverse at present, can only enrich itself from new significations and unforeseen developments within the evolution of a dynamic situation which will see the fall of the capitalist social relation. It is thus not only the responses to the communizing problematic, i.e. practices, which will be modified with the arrival of a revolutionary period, but also the questions posed. Every contemporary practice which would like to be communizing must therefore recognize that it *responds inadequately to a badly posed question;* which at the same time subtracts nothing from its value. For the question and its answer are inadequate to serve as the measure of that which the future of communism as a universal social relation could be; but they are completely adequate to give to contemporary struggles a meaning that they wouldn't possess without them, and which can reveal itself as subsequently determinant for the possibility of producing communism.

To want to wage a struggle whilst freeing oneself from all mediations put in place by capital (unions, politics, media, law, etc.) is an obvious example of a manner of posing questions which treat of communization.[39] Indeed – why not? – searching for a collective life and 'different' relations, on the condition that they are in the context of as struggle, can also be an example.

Clearly all experimental practices are not for that reason communist, and they can even be taken up in a sense which has no communizing sense, as forms simply rehabilitated in a purely capitalist framework. This is exactly the case with squats which were at a certain moment a response in terms of organization and everyday life to a number of similar questions, but which can just as easily be one place of artistic promotion among others. The same for general assemblies, workers' councils, factory occupations, etc. All these forms of struggle can be, at a given moment, a response to a communizing problematic, as they can be the contrary. The hypostasis of one of these forms can only become an ideology.

Quarto decimo

To the formula of *Call* which says: 'the overthrowing of capitalism will come from those who are able to create the conditions for other types of relations,' we must respond: 'the conditions for other types of relations will be created by those who are able to overthrow capitalism.'

(translation: Endnotes.)

Frames of Struggle

Now and Never
Alberto Toscano

In recent years, the ideas of common, communism and commune have come to occupy the radical political imagination, achieving a certain circulation and even gaining a foothold in what one could call the spontaneous philosophy or common sense of some political activism. These concepts have been given different, sometimes incommensurable, inflections by various authors and schools of thought, but their current prominence and diffusion may be regarded as indicative of a lowered tolerance for a social order whose returns are ever-diminishing, and whose future appears ever bleaker. But they also register the lack, or the refusal, of a 'classical' revolutionary image of emancipation that would identify the subjects and mechanisms capable of transforming this world into another one.

There is a curious trait shared by many disparate, and often mutually hostile, branches of contemporary anticapitalist theory: the epochal defeats of workers' and communist movements are recoded as preconditions or signs of a possible victory. Whether deindustrialisation is viewed as a response to the emancipatory flight of labor from the factory or the collapse of the party-form is welcomed as heralding a truly generic communism unburdened from bureaucratic authority, today's partisans of a communism reloaded detect signs of hope in the social and political realities that pushed scores into renegacy or despair. The title of a collection of texts by the group *Tiqqun* – *Everything's Failed, Long Live Communism!*[40] – could serve as the motto for much thinking in this vein. On one level, there is nothing particularly novel about this: the stagnation, betrayal or collapse of official socialisms or Marxisms has frequently been perceived by dissident communists (councilists, Trotskyists, situationists, workerists, etc.) as the occasion for re-establishing their practice on a theoretically firm and politically coherent platform, away from the disastrous compromises and collusions that marred the mainstream.[41] Indeed, declaring the foreignness to a true communism of the hegemonic organizations in the workers' movement and of socialist states was the *raison d'être* of many of the political traditions that formed those thinkers who today continue to proclaim themselves communists.[42]

To different degrees, an expatriated Marxism and a hypothetical communism characterise much of the theoretical panorama of the radical Left.[43] But what is it to be a theoretical heretic after the political death of orthodoxy? This is not an otiose question: being orphaned of one's overbearing and intimate enemy (the dominant communist and workers' movement), has marked a watershed in the interlinked histories of dissident communisms. Though, as indicated by the periodic exorcisms of the determinist Marxist bogeyman, the habits of opposition die hard, the discursive domain in which contemporary theoretical communisms exists is a markedly different one than it was even a couple of decades ago. Significantly, the separation from the deadening weight of the Soviet monolith has not translated into the much-vaunted liberation of political energies that many on the far Left announced around 1989. Central to the critical repertoire of dissident communists towards the official movement was the claim that the latter had abandoned the project of revolution, that for all of its own condemnations of the limits of social-democracy and the dangers of opportunism, it had sunk into a sterile gradualism (in the capitalist countries) or perpetuated capitalism itself under conditions of bureaucratic domination (in the socialist ones).

Among the features of this dissidence without orthodoxy is the struggle to generate a contemporary concept of revolution, accompanied by the tendency to refuse the idea that anything like reform is possible in the present (contrary to the kind of gradualist positions that would see a domestication of capitalism, say by the regulation of financial transaction, or some neo-Keynesian compromise, as both viable and desirable). In fact, I would suggest that the seemingly inexorable collapse of any reformist project, together with the adulteration of 'reform' into a concept synonymous with neoliberal adjustment (as in 'pension reform'), has had remarkably deep effects on the radical political imagination, and on its very vocabulary. The upshot of this predicament is the proliferation of an intransitive politics – by which I mean the idea of emancipation and equality no longer as objectives of a drawn-out programme, a strategy and/or a transition, but as matters of immediate practice, in a fusion of means and ends that seems to abrogate the entire temporal framework of reform and revolution.

The parameters of the classical distinction between reform and revolution – present, for instance, in Rosa Luxemburg's famous polemic against Eduard Bernstein[44] – appear to have fallen by the wayside. Social-democratic reformism was founded on a theory of capitalism's (more or less limitless) capacities for adaptation, whose tendencies to crisis would be neutralized by credit, the unification of capitals and the perfecting of the means of communication, opening up the possibility for a reformist path to socialism through unionization, social reforms and the democratization of the state – that is on a theory of the virtuous dialectic in the capital-labor relation, whose temporality one could discern in the post-war Fordism of the Golden Thirties. For Luxemburg, not only was such adaptation illusory (and we could easily turn our minds today to the vicious rather than virtuous relation between credit, communication and big capital) but the revolutionary perspective necessitates the eventuality of a *collapse* of capitalism, a collapse both assumed and accelerated by conscious revolutionary masses. In this light, the loss of a theory tying together the time of action and the materiality of history renders certain contemporary debates on communism more formal than strategic.

That the tentative recovery of the political idea of communism in the present should take an a- or even anti-historical form should be no surprise to the historical materialist. At an uneven and global scale, the bond between the temporality of capitalist development and that of class struggle and formation, joined with the reflux of the labor movement, organized revolutionary politics and of anti-imperial liberation struggles means that the idea of an egalitarian overcoming of the capitalist mode of production, written inexorably into the latter's tendency, has little if any mobilising power or plausibility. It is symptomatic that even those who seek to maintain, in however mutant a guise, a notion of capitalism as the bearer of real propensities towards alternate forms of production, association and sociality explicitly forsake the language of history, often in the guise of a repudiation of political memory and a critique of teleology – a *forma mentis* that when repressed tends to return more or less surreptitiously, for instance in the guise of various forms of spontaneous, insurgent, or reticular revolution, which more or less contend that emancipation is latent in social trends. This optimism of reason is not so widespread, however, and I would suggest that the critical or anticapitalist common sense is that there are no immanent tendencies or dispositions that augur a transition, save, and this is hardly encouraging, the barbaric or nihilistic propensities of a capitalism that is increasingly exclusionary of an unemployed and surplus humanity, and menacingly, and for some irreversibly, destructive of the very natural basis for human social existence.

For all of its internal variations and differends, the current radical or communist renascence in theory can thus be negatively characterised by the apparent abeyance of the reform/revolution dyad, and by the concurrent problematization of the progressive schema of communism's overcoming of capitalism, which in classical Marxisms was politically translated into various imaginaries and strategies of transition, be they reformist or revolutionary. Two things can be noted at this point. The first is that the loss of the theoretical schema that tied together capitalist development, capitalist crisis, class subjectivity and political organization into a strategic and temporal framework – 'reform or revolution' (or even revolutionary reforms, or non-reformist reforms) – means that the field in which contemporary communist theorists stake their political positions has uncertain contours. Intransigent opposition to the perpetuation of capitalist relations of exploitation and domination coexists with proposed measures (from the social wage to the unconditional regularization of all 'illegal' workers) which do not fit into the politics of time of classical Marxism, being neither revolutionary instruments nor tactical expedients, neither strategic steps nor elements of a transitional programme. The second very significant feature of the recent discussion of communism (as well as of related terms like common and commune) is the manner in which the loss or repudiation of the historico-political imaginary of the overcoming of capitalism, that is, the generation of an a- or anti-historical communism, has been accompanied by historicizing reflections explaining why the transitive politics of the nineteenth and twentieth centuries (whether reformist or revolutionary) has become obsolescent. Here too, the essence of defeat appears to be a kind of victory: only now, with the thoroughgoing post-Fordist restructuring and decomposition of the industrial working class is a politics of species-being possible; or, in a different vein, it is the saturation of the political sequences linked to class and party, which at last allows us to revive an 'invariant' communist idea, in which the affirmation of equality is not subordinated to the imperatives and instrumentalities of power; or again, it is with the planetary expansion of a neoliberalism hell-bent on accumulation by dispossession that we can recognize the defence, reconstitution and production of commons as the transversal and transhistorical impetus of a communism at last unburdened of stageism,

Eurocentrism and a technophilic productivism.

With the foregoing, and admittedly impressionistic, theoretical sketch, I wanted to provide a context of sorts, if not necessarily for the formulation of a theory of communisation (which has its own genealogies in the European ultra-Left[45]) then at least for its reception. Whether we view them as profound conjunctural commonalities, family resemblances or misleading surface-effects (I would opt for the first), there are affinities worthy of note between a kind of communist *air du temps* and the specific theoretical proposals of Théorie Communiste (TC), Troploin, Endnotes and others. From an external, and broadly diagnostic position – such as the one taken here, in what is not a contribution to communization theory itself – the existence of a broad set of contemporary theoretical proposals staking a claim to communism but refusing the politics of transition is of considerable significance, even if the reasons for promoting an intransitive communism or the visions of political action consequent upon it may differ widely.

There is no denying that the refusal of a transitional understanding of communist politics, and the related historicization of that refusal in terms of the theory of real subsumption and the analysis of 'programmatism' (on which see the essays by Theorié Communiste and Endnotes in this volume) make the position outlined by communization theory both unique and uniquely reflexive relative to the theoretical panorama sketched above. What's more, in conjunction with what appear to be a root-and-branch jettisoning of the *political* legacies of the workers' and socialist movements, there is a much greater degree of fidelity to a certain Marxian *theoretical* framework. Thus, class and revolution remain unequivocally in the foreground of TC and Endnotes texts, and the classic, if very often neglected, conception of communism as the real movement of the destruction of capitalist social relations, of the abolition of the value-form, is at the center of their reflections. Both the promise and the limitations of communization theory, are to be found, to my mind, in this conjunction of value-theoretical rigor and political repudiation of Marxist and communist traditions, the ultra-Left ones included.

In what follows, I want to dwell on the problems I discern in the political, or better anti-political, dimensions of communization theory, approaching their complex and in many ways compelling analyses of value and class struggle from the vantage point of the rejection of the politics of transition. Inevitably, this will mean providing a truncated critique of arguments that have the considerable virtue of operating at the level of the totality, though I would maintain that the paucity of strategic and political reflection within communization theory is debilitating notwithstanding, or in the end perhaps because of, the coherence of its theoretical analyses.

Let us take two definitions of communization, from TC and Endnotes respectively:

> In the course of revolutionary struggle, the abolition of the state, of exchange, of the division of labor, of all forms of property, the extension of the situation where everything is freely available as the unification of human activity – in a word, the abolition of classes – are 'measures' that abolish capital, imposed by the very necessities of struggle against the capitalist class. The revolution is communization; it does not have communism as a project and result, but as its very content.[46]
>
> Communization is the destruction of the commodity-form and the simultaneous establishment of immediate social relations between individuals. Value, understood as a total form of social mediation, cannot be got rid of by halves.[47]

Some salient features of communization theory can be drawn from these definitions: the refusal of a separation between means and ends in revolutionary practice; the idea that revolution is directly aimed at the value-form and the capital-relation; the immediacy of both revolution and of the social relations it generates. These propositions stress the radical novelty and negativity of communism when considered in the context of the present. Unlike many of their contemporaries, the theorists of communization, while affirming the historical immanence of communist possibilities against any (overtly or crypto-humanist) vision of communism's invariance,[48] refuse to countenance the notion that embryos or zones of communism exist in the present. This is in many respects a virtue, especially in contrast to the shallow optimism of those who claim we've already won the world, but simply need to shake off the husk of capitalist domination. But the salutary emphasis on communism as the real movement of the destruction of value as a social form risks trading off theoretical coherence and purity for practical irrelevance. The Leninist catechism once had it that there's no revolutionary movement without revolutionary theory. It would be a bitter irony if the refinement of revolutionary theory made revolutionary practice inconceivable.

With the aim of sounding out the political limits of the anti-political character of communization theory, I want to indicate some domains of communist theorizing, both classical and contemporary, which communization theory disavows at its peril. Let us call these, in order, problems of communist strategy, of communist power, of communist culture and of communist transition.

If something marks out the contemporary resurgence of theoretical interest in communism, across its various species, it is the almost total neglect of the question of strategy. The organizational reasons are obvious enough: the collapse or attenuation of those collective bodies that could project a path for a subject through space and time, and in the face of adverse structures and subjects, makes strategic thought largely residual or speculative (unless we include those entities, namely the Chinese Communist Party, whose largely successful strategy has involved jettisoning allegiance to communist principles). But there are also historical sources for the waning of strategy:

all the subversive strategies have both borrowed and reversed the political categories of modernity: sovereignty, but democratic and popular; citizenship, but social; territorial liberation and internationalism; war, but popular war. So it is not surprising that the crisis of the political paradigm of modernity is mirrored by the crisis in the strategies of subversion, beginning with the overturning of all their spatiotemporal conditions.[49]

The collusion of modern forms of political abstraction with value's domination and commensuration of human activity can also account for why communization theory presents us with a trenchantly non- or anti-modern (but certainly not postmodern) Marxism.

But can we abandon strategy along with political modernity? When communization theorists address the question of politics, which is to say of revolution (a notion they have the consistency to put at the front and center of their theorizing, unlike most of their contemporaries), they do so on the basis of a curious presupposition: to wit, that a struggle which is directly and uncompromisingly targeted at the abolition of capitalist value-relations is the only kind capable of bringing about communist victory. This anti-strategic strategy – which consciously repudiates the entire panoply of strategic reflection in the communist camp, from class alliance to tactical retreat, from united front to seizure of power – seems to me to confuse a historical judgment with a theoretical proposition. The judgment is widespread enough: all efforts at communism that did not venture immediately to abolish value-relations and concomitantly to abolish the revolutionary class itself were defeated, mutated into bureaucratic despotisms, or were recuperated into capitalism (even as its unlikely 'saviors', as in today's China). With considerable orthodoxy, and echoing the Engels of *The Peasant War in Germany*, TC have argued (against the voluntarist strain of communization theory of Nesic & Dauvé or Troploin), that these setbacks were written into the history of subsumption, rather than amounting to simple subjective or organizational failings.

One could of course counter, as I would be tempted to, that just because a problem (that of communist strategy, or of transition) has not been solved, does not mean it was the wrong problem all along. But even if we accepted the premises of communization theory, there is no argument presented as to how communization could amount to a *successful* strategy. Given that, by the communization theorists' own lights, there are even fewer (that is, *no*) examples of communization than of transition as actually existing practices, it is obscure on what grounds, other than the historical failures of their contraries, we are to accept that the *immediate* negation of capitalist relations is the best path towards the *effective* negation of capitalist relations. Why the collapse of capitalist forms of social reproduction, the avowed consequence of communization, would herald the construction of communist social relations, rather than the collapse of social reproduction tout court, we are not told. Similarly, in what regard the refusal of the separation between the military, the social and the political, could serve revolutionary communizing movements in struggles against highly centralized and differentiated martial and repressive apparatuses with seemingly limitless capabilities for organized violence remains a mystery. Even if we accept that all transitional strategies are doomed, this does not in any way suggest that intransitive, anti-strategic varieties of communism have any better chances of dislocating the domination of the value-form – far from it. The rather fanciful descriptions of revolutionary activity in some writings on communization suggest that, faced with the extremely unlikely (or impossible) prospect of a politics capable of living up to its standards of coherent negation, it will slip into a kind of tragic fatalism, in which no revolutionary practice will ever overcome the stringent constraints of revolutionary theory.

As an important corollary to this problem of strategy, it should be noted that the totalizing linearity of the conception of the history of real subsumption proposed by communization theory results in a presentation of the current conjuncture as one in which capital's production of sameness has rendered the questions of spatial, cultural, and geopolitical difference obsolete. The narrative of the mutations of the class-relation, of workers' identity, and of their political manifestations (namely, as 'programmatism'), together with the axiom that communization must spread like the proverbial planetary prairie fire or simply not be, appear to depend on the extrapolation of an already streamlined Euro-American history to the whole globe. The idea that class formation may still be occurring elsewhere,[50] with different shapes and in different rhythms, is rejected, as is the entire conceptualization, which we owe to a historico-geographical materialism of the *necessarily* uneven and combined development of capitalism, and with it of struggle in and against it.[51] Rather than confronting the problems that beset the construction of effective solidarities across polities, and especially across a transnational division of labor which is employed by capital for ends at once disciplinary and exploitative, communization theory takes its account of real subsumption as warrant to sideline all of these problems, thereby ignoring precisely those very real obstacles which demand strategic reflection instead of the rather unscientific presupposition that everything will be resolved in the struggle.

Among the obvious components of any strategic thought is the element of power. Advance or retreat, patience or urgency, concentration or dispersal – the options taken depend largely on estimations of power, be it material, moral or military. But communization theory seems to hold this concern in little regard. The coercive excrescence of the state, the shifting capabilities of groups, action on the action of others, the shaping of political subjectivities by social mechanisms and ideologies – these issues are absorbed by the systemic periodization of class (de)composition and class struggle. Is this because the theories of transition that characterized 'programmatism' were all predicated on calculating the power of the class, and judging the context and timing of its political action? Be it in the formation of popular or united fronts, for reasons of stageism or expediency, or in the theorization of revolutionary dual power as the vanishing mediator on the path to overthrowing the capitalist state,[52] the question of the organized capacity for antagonism loomed large. Again, whatever the historical and political judgment passed on these specific strategies, it is difficult to see how, on pain of a self-defeating voluntarism, the question of class power wouldn't arise, even or especially in communizing processes. When, how, with whom and with what to undertake communization is surely not an otiose question. Short of treating the historical mutations of the class-relation as themselves the sources of class power, the power to undertake communization (something that would smack of 'historical mysticism'[53]), communization theory, as a thoroughgoing theory of emancipation from capital's abstract domination, cannot do without some theory of power. What's more, unless we treat the capabilities of the state as themselves entirely subsumed by capital, something that seems unpersuasive given the different articulations of state(s) and capital(s) on the present scene, it would appear necessary to consider the relevance, for strategic purposes, and thus for the particular shape taken by communizing activity, of the distinction between economic and extra-economic coercion. The obstacles to communization may, for instance, take explicitly repressive or co-optive forms, just as the capital-relation reproduces itself through the gun, the ballot-box and the spectacle. If communization is to be more than a formalistic theory or a pure (which is to say metaphysical) activity, that is, if it is to translate into strategy, these differences will surely matter.

In the present panorama of anticapitalisms, communization theory stands out for the insistence with which it refuses the consolations of the enclave or the pieties of the alternative. In its nigh-on ascetic fixation on the abolition of the value-form as the *sine qua non* of communist theory and practice, it regards with (mostly warranted) suspicion the proliferation of positions which hold that we can struggle in the present in ways which prefigure a post-capitalist future. Among the analytical attractions of communization theory is the way in which it permits us to historicize and critique recent attempts, in the context of the widespread opposition to neoliberalism and globalization (terms which often substitute for, rather than specify, capitalism), to envisage immanent alternatives to capitalism. Unwittingly, such positions – advocacies of global transitional demands like the Tobin Tax or efforts to create liberated zones, temporary or otherwise – place themselves within, and are limited by, the reproduction of the class-relation, whether they disavow the very notion of class (struggle) or not. Such 'radical democratisms' can be faulted for regarding the saving of capitalism from itself as the only path to emancipation, an emancipation that turns out to require the perpetuation of the fundamental framework of exploitation.[54]

It is to the credit of communization theorists like TC that they do not advocate, on the basis of their critiques of *theories* of reform, alternative, or transition, a withdrawal from the concrete forms that present struggles take, including those which, inevitably, have as their stakes the defense of certain forms of reproduction (the welfare state). But re-marking the limit of contemporary conceptions of alternatives to capitalism cannot exempt a theory of communism from thinking through how to foster and fashion those capacities that would make the disarticulation of capitalist relations and the establishment of communist ones possible. Aside from functioning as an antidote to the inertia of means that make emancipatory ends recede into a distant horizon, the strength of the prefigurative conception of communism[55] is to pose the problem of how in (capitalist) social relations as they now exist, one can experiment and prepare the tools for its overcoming. Such prefiguration (for instance, to take a very minor but pertinent case, in the internal functioning of a theoretical group) need not conceive itself as a 'liberated zone', but could be advanced as the inevitably truncated, imperfect and embryonic testing out of certain practices, whose role in future struggles may be undefined, but which at the very least begins to explore the creation of collective organs of opposition.

The fact that communization theory treats the overcoming of instrumentality only in the struggle itself – in the guise of communizing measures inseparable from communist aims – leads to a strangely empty formalism, which tells us next to nothing about the forms that the negation of capitalist relations could take, as if not-capitalism and communism were synonymous. The positing that real subsumption has put a labor without reserves at last into the position where self-abolition is the only object – a positing illustrated by a tendentious sampling of 'pure' negations (riots, strikes without demands, etc.), treating any resurgences of 'traditional' organizations of the workers' movement as merely residual – translates into the view that nothing needs to be done to *prepare* the kind of subjects that might take communizing action. The realization that dogged many a twentieth-century communist theorist – to wit, that capital is based not just on a social form, but on deeply sedimented, somatized and interiorized habits and reflexes – is ignored in the bleakly optimistic view that all will be resolved in the struggle, and not before, by the cascading and contagious negation of all instances of the capital-relation. Whatever our historical judgment on them may be, I would submit instead that the problem of building a proletarian capacity before a revolutionary moment, posed most comprehensively by Gramsci,[56] or that of building a communist culture, which occupied militants, theorists and artists in the immediate wake of the Bolshevik revolution, remain with us as problems. The mutation or collapse of a working-class identity in its nineteenth and twentieth-century guises only renders this question of experimenting with non-capitalist forms of life (without reifying them into quickly atrophied 'free zones') more urgent. And even if we shy away from the capital-pessimism that would see total commodification triumphant, we can nevertheless readily admit that not just labor, but also much of our everyday life has been subsumed by capital in a way that puts many a complex obstacle in the way of building up the capacity and the intelligence to negate it.

To have forcefully emphasized and rigorously investigated two indispensable elements of communist theory – the character of capitalism as a system of abstract domination based on the value-form and the vision of communism as the revolutionary self-abolition of the proletariat – is a great credit to communization theory. That it has tried to think these elements in their unity, and to do so with an attention to the present possibilities of emancipation, as well as its historical trajectory, makes it a position worth engaging with for anyone preoccupied with the question of communism as a contemporary one. But the stringency of its critiques of the communist tradition has not translated into a reflexive investigation of the consequences attendant on abandoning any concept of transition, and of the kinds of strategy and forms of political organization that may be up to the task of a contemporary transition. No more than similar professions of faith in the party or the productive forces from other quarters, the exegete's mantra that communism is nothing but the movement of the abolition of the status quo should not be taken as a license to ignore the *whom* and *how* of any revolutionary process, laying all trust in a kind of learning-by-doing that seems wantonly indifferent to the gargantuan obstacles in the way of negating capital. In social, economic and political spaces amply subsumed by the value-form you can't make it up as you go along. The path is not made by walking it, but will require some pretty detailed surveying of political forces, weak points, and perhaps most significantly, a sustained reflection how to turn the accreted dead labor of humanity into a resource for living labor, even as it abolishes itself *qua* labor.[57] It is a methodological error to presume that the real abstraction that can be registered at the level of a history of subsumption trumps the concrete uses of spatial and material differences by capital (and labor), and that we can directly translate value theory into a diagnosis of the present.

Even if we accept a variant of the real subsumption thesis, this will never mean the real obsolescence of the unevennesses, differences and mediations which make it possible for capitalism to function. The triumph of value is not the death of politics, or the extinction of strategy. Reversing the valence of a term from Whitehead, we could speak with respect of communization theory of a fallacy of misplaced abstraction, which takes the intensification and extension of the capital-relation as eliminating, rather than refunctioning, politics. The obverse of this anti-strategic treatment of capitalist abstraction is the conception of communization as the immediate (in both senses of the term) negation of capitalism. But the homogenizing characterization of capitalism's social abstraction, and the treatment of its further mediations (ideology, political forms, class fractions) as of little moment, means that the negation proposed by communization theory is poor in determinations.

This appears to derive from two main factors. The first is the hopeful conviction, already alluded to in regard to the problem of strategy, that such determinations will simply arise in the collective processes of abolishing the value-form. I can see no reason to have such confidence, especially in light of the formidable organizational and logistical difficulties that face any attempt to undo the ubiquitous identification of social existence and capitalist mediation – not to mention the often catastrophic challenges previously confronted by really-existing communisms. The second factor is the entirely untenable notion that communism involves 'direct social relations'. As authors from Fourier to Harvey have suggested, it makes much more sense to conceive a non-capitalist future as one that will involve infinitely more varied and more complex forms of social mediation, forms for which the refunctioning of many (though definitely not all) of the devices which permit the reproduction of capital will be necessary. If the world we inhabit is one that has been thoroughly shaped by the history of capital (and of class struggle), it stands to reason that simple negation – with its tendency to facile fantasies of communism rising like a phoenix from the ashes of anomie and the thorough collapse of social reproduction – is no proposal at all. In a world where no object or relation is untouched by capital, the logistical, strategic and political question is in many ways what will require abolishing, and what converting, or, in a more dialectical vein, what is to be negated without remainder and what sublated. If real subsumption is second nature, and New York City a natural fact,[58] then a communizing movement will need to experiment with how to transform a world in which relations of exploitation and domination are present all the way down. It will need to dominate domination with the aim of non-domination. This is a problem at once material – a question of buildings, chemicals, ports, power-grids, train-lines, pharmaceuticals, and so on and so forth – and of necessity temporal.

How can we redeem and redirect our dead labors? How can we control the very systems that control us, without allowing their deeply embedded capitalist and dominative potentialities to assert themselves? Negation alone is not going to do the job. And a refusal of the sober realism that accepts the necessary alienation[59] and inevitable hierarchy of certain systems, as well as the inevitable continuation of capitalist forms in post-capitalist futures,[60] will simply return communism to the melancholy domain of the idea or the enclave. The problem of transition will not go away by fiat. The question is not *whether* communism requires a thinking of transition, but *which* transition, or transitions, have any chance in the present.

5

Capitalism: Some Disassembly Required
Nicole Pepperell

Marx aims to present an immanent critique of the reproduction of capital. He aims, in other words, to show how the process by which capital is reproduced necessarily also reproduces the potential for the emancipatory transformation of capitalist society. In the *Grundrisse*, Marx uses the metaphor of mines that are ready to explode capitalist production from within, suggesting that emancipatory social movements mobilize an arsenal that has been inadvertently built by the very social practices they seek to transform:

> [W]ithin bourgeois society, the society that rests on *exchange value*, there arise relations of circulation as well as of production which are so many mines to explode it. (A mass of antithetical forms of the social unity, whose antithetical character can never be abolished through quiet metamorphosis. On the other hand, if we did not find concealed in society as it is the material conditions of production and the corresponding relations of exchange prerequisite for a classless society, then all attempts to explode it would be quixotic.)[61]

But how does Marx understand the generation of such explosive possibilities? By what means does the reproduction of capital necessarily reproduce the potential for alternative forms of collective life? Different answers have been proposed by the Marxist tradition.

Three approaches to understanding emancipatory potential

Two of these answers can be positioned on opposing sides of a dichotomy. On one side are approaches that emphasize how capitalism generates *objective* potentials for transformation – through the development of the forces of production, whose technical and social character drives a progression toward socialized forms of ownership and democratic forms of self-government. On the other side are approaches that focus more on how capitalism generates *subjective* potentials for transformation – through its dependence on an ever-expanding proletarian class whose material interests oppose the social relations on which capitalist production is based, and whose centrality to material production provides both emancipatory insight and transformative power.

Both of these approaches came under fire in the 20th century, as fascist mass movements and the development of totalitarian planned economies were interpreted as evidence that neither subjective nor objective conditions suffice to drive social transformation to emancipatory ends. One response to this historical experience was a turn to theories of 'social forms' – structured patterns of social practice that are understood to determine both objective and subjective dimensions of capitalist societies. Contemporary social form theories generally point back to Lukács' seminal 'Reification and the Consciousness of the Proletariat', which portrays capitalist society as a 'totality' whose structures of subjectivity and objectivity are determined by the commodity form:

> ... at this stage in the history of mankind there is no problem that does not ultimately lead back to that question and there is no

solution that could not be found in the solution to the riddle of the commodity-*structure*... the problem of commodities must not be considered in isolation or even regarded as the central problem in economics, but as the central structural problem of capitalist society is all its aspects. Only in this case can the structure of commodity-relations be made to yield a model of all the objective forms of bourgeois society together with all the subjective forms corresponding to them.[62]

At first glance, theories of social form appear greatly to increase the depth and sophistication of Marx's work. They reposition *Capital* as a general theory of modernity, rather than a narrow 'economic' analysis, and they apply this theory to culture, psychological structure, governmental forms, and many other dimensions of social life. They also appear to account better for the difficulties facing transformative social movements, suggesting that such movements must wrestle with an internal battle against their members' psyches, a symbolic battle against their cultures, and an institutional battle against forms of production and government that are all fundamentally shaped by the same core social forms.

Yet the very strength of such approaches in accounting for the failure of revolutionary expectations has arguably handicapped them in the search for emancipatory possibilities. Since Lukács, theories of social form have tended to look *through* the diversity of social practice in order to pick out an underlying formal pattern. Such theories are thus tacitly reductive – granting a privileged status to formal patterns visible beneath the flux of everyday social practice, while implicitly treating the diversity of social practice as epiphenomenal. This problem is related to the tendency for theories of social form to remain untethered from an analysis of how the formal pattern is *produced*. This both presumes that it is possible to define the form without a concrete analysis of its production – an assumption with which Marx would have strongly disagreed – and also tends to propel the analysis into idealist forms.

In the versions of social form theory dominant today, this latent idealism is expressed in several different forms: as pessimism;[63] as a claim that capital genuinely exhibits 'idealist' properties;[64] or as the claim that the forms are 'quasi-autonomous' from the social actors who create them.[65] While theories of social form often assert the possibility for emancipatory transformation – and even argue that this potential should be associated with dimensions of social life that cannot be fully characterized by formal structures – the failure to theorize the determinate properties of these other dimensions of social life, or to analyze how the social forms are generated, tends to render theories of social form essentially exhortative. Their relative sophistication does not extend to the theorization of concrete emancipatory possibilities.

So was the turn to social form theories a dead end? Would a return to theories of objective or subjective potential provide a better starting point for grasping concrete possibilities for social transformation? I argue below that Marx's work suggests another alternative: a non-reductive theory of how concrete social practices operate in tandem to generate overarching patterns of historical change (social forms), while also and simultaneously generating a diverse array of determinate possibilities for alternative forms of collective life.

Political Economy as Intelligent Design

In the opening chapter of *Capital*, in a rare explicit methodological discussion, Marx credits the political economists precisely for their insight into the social forms that characterize capitalist production:

> Political economy has indeed analyzed value and its magnitude, however incompletely, and has uncovered the content concealed within these forms. But it has never once asked the question why this content has assumed that particular form, that is to say, why labor is expressed in value, and why the measurement of labor

by its duration is expressed in the magnitude of the value of the product. These formulas, which bear the unmistakable stamp of belonging to a social formation in which the process of production has mastery over man, instead of the opposite, appear to the political economists' bourgeois consciousness to be as much a self-evident and nature-imposed necessity as productive labor itself.[66]

This passage suggests that Marx does not regard the discovery of social forms to be his distinctive contribution to the critique of political economy. Instead, he singles out the question of how content comes to assume a specific form – which is to say, how a specific set of social forms themselves are produced.

He argues that, by contrast, the political economists stop short, evidently awestruck by the presence of structured patterns that appear to them to emerge 'spontaneously' from a chaotic array of social practices, none of which is intentionally undertaken with the goal of producing this specific aggregate result. Apologistically, the political economists take the emergence of this unexpected, unplanned order to imply that an underlying rationality governs capitalist production. How else could order arise in the absence of conscious design, unless current forms of production were somehow tapping into the underlying natural order that latently governs material production?

For this reason, the political economists are able to declare capitalist production 'natural', and all previous forms of production 'artificial' – in spite of their knowledge that capitalist institutions are recent historical developments. The emergence of an unplanned order – the apparent 'intelligibility' of capitalist production, demonstrated by the political economists' ability to discover non-random trends beneath the chaotic flux of everyday social practice – is taken as a sign that this historically specific mode of production has been ratified by Nature and Reason.

Marx is scathing towards this apologist conclusion. He compares the political economists to the Church fathers, and accuses them of treating their own historically contingent social institutions as an 'emanation of God':

> The economists have a singular way of proceeding. For them, there are only two kinds of institutions, artificial and natural. The institutions of feudalism are artificial institutions, those of the bourgeoisie are natural institutions. In this they resemble the theologians, who likewise establish two kinds of religion. Every religion which is not [t]heirs is an invention of men, while their own is an emanation of God... Thus there has been history, but there is no longer any.[67]

With this passage, Marx declares that his project – much like Darwin's – is driven by the desire to explain the emergence of a particular kind of order, without falling back on mystical concepts of an intelligent designer, a *Geist*, or an invariant Natural Law.

From Marx's perspective, political economy is only nominally secular. It may invoke the mantle of science and enlightened self-understanding, but it responds with a distinctly uncritical amazement when confronted by structured patterns of historical change that arise independently from conscious human will. This amazement is expressed in the unwarranted conclusion that the presence of unintentional order is evidence of the rationality or goodness of the system within which this order becomes manifest.

In *Capital*, Marx presents an alternative analysis of the process of 'spontaneous self-organization' that reproduces capital. Marx portrays the reproduction of capital as a blind and oppressive juggernaut, accidentally generated as an unintentional side effect of a wide array of different social practices, none of which is directly oriented to achieving this aggregate result. This juggernaut may not be *random* – it may be characterized by theorizable trends and demonstrable forms of orderly historical change – and this non-random character may make it *intelligible* – it may be subject to systematic theorization. This intelligibility, however, does not make the process *rational* in the sense of reflecting a desirable outcome from our collective social practice. The non-random character of the process cannot be taken as evidence that something beneficial will result if we allow this process to operate free of human interference. Marx attempts to show that a number of non-beneficial consequences will predictably be generated, so long as capital continues to be reproduced. At the same time, he tries to demystify the process of capital's reproduction by cataloguing the makeshift assemblage of contingent social practices that must operate in tandem to generate this 'spontaneous, self-organizing' process.

Through this analysis Marx seeks to invert the conventional 'enlightened' narrative of political economy in two ways. First, Marx severs the enlightenment connection between law and reason, by demonstrating how a blind and accidental process could arise from purely contingent human behaviours and yet still manifest lawlike qualities. Second, Marx contests the political desirability of grounding normative standards in the 'spontaneous' trends of capitalist production. He argues that the reproduction of capital does generate emancipatory possibilities – but he insists that these are hindered by capitalism's spontaneous trends: deliberate political action is required to wrest emancipatory potentials from the process by which capital is reproduced.

Marx pursues these goals by cataloguing what he calls the 'microscopic anatomy' of capitalist production.[68] This catalogue is intended to produce a systematic theory of the forms of internal social variability that must necessarily be generated, if capital is to continue to be reproduced. This necessary internal variability then becomes key to Marx's argument that it is possible to speciate a new, more emancipatory, form of collective life by selectively inheriting already existing social potentials, in order to produce new institutions that are better adapted to emancipatory ends. To understand how this analysis plays out in *Capital*, we must take a brief detour through Marx's idiosyncratic presentational style.

'The Higher Realms of Nonsense'

In an often-quoted passage from the postface to the second German edition of *Capital*, Marx famously distinguishes between his own method of inquiry – the forms of analysis he used to arrive at his conclusions – and his method of presentation – the way he displays his argument in *Capital*:

> Of course the method of presentation must differ in form from that of inquiry. The latter has to appropriate the material in detail, to analyze its different forms of development and to track down their inner connection. Only after this work has been done can the real movement be appropriately presented. If this is done successfully, if the life of the subject-matter is now reflected back in the ideas, then it may appear as if we have before us an *a priori* construction.[69]

While the passage is well-known, its implications for reading *Capital* are generally not fully appreciated. *Capital* does not give us – immediately and on the surface – an account of Marx's own analytical procedure. Instead, what the text presents most immediately is a 'method of presentation'. But what does this mean?

When we open the first chapter of *Capital* and begin reading what we see first is a sort of arm-chair empiricist sociological analysis. This analysis invites us to take a look at the 'elementary form' of the wealth of capitalist societies, and proceeds to break down the characteristics of this form, dividing it into use-value and exchange-value.[70] We do not know at this point what Marx is presenting, what function this analysis might serve. What we do know is that this analysis does not reflect Marx's own personal method of inquiry. The form of reasoning and analysis displayed in these opening passages – whatever it is for – is not intended to illustrate a recommended means of arriving at critical sociological insights. It is, instead, part of Marx's method of presentation. We need to keep this in mind, bracket the question of what is being presented for the moment, and move on.

In a couple of pages, the text invites us to 'consider the matter more closely'[71] – by contrast, that is, to the sort of analysis with which the text started. We still do not know why we are being asked to do this – but we do know, now, that the analysis with which we were initially presented must somehow be too superficial. Otherwise, why would we need to consider the matter more closely?

The text now presents a new analysis of the wealth of capitalist societies – one that moves beyond the text's empiricist beginnings to present a very strange sort of transcendental argument, which purports to logically deduce the necessity for a 'supersensible' category beyond use-value and exchange-value: the category of value. It builds on this deduction to infer the need for the category of abstract labor, and then to analyze some of the properties of these new categories.[72]

Many of the claims made in this section seem quite counter-intuitive, and the form of argument seems profoundly problematic. Both critics and supporters of Marx have expressed incredulity at these passages, baffled at why Marx is putting forward this analysis.[73] This bafflement arises because readers take these passages to exemplify Marx's own method of inquiry.

At the beginning of the third section of the chapter, Marx uses a quick reference to Shakespeare to mock the forms of analysis that have just been on display. He compares political economy unfavorably to Dame Quickly, asserting that political economy does not know 'where to have' its categories: 'The objectivity of commodities as values differs from Dame Quickly in the sense that "a man knows not where to have it."'[74] The reference here is a crude sexual innuendo – Marx is impugning the analytical virility of the political economists by implying that they are unable to bed down their categories properly. The previous sections have left the ontological status of the wealth of capitalist society unclear: is it the straightforward, empirical object with which we started the chapter? Or the immaterial transcendental essence to which we later moved? If we had found ourselves identifying with either of these forms of analysis, the Dame Quickly joke breaks the spell. Both of these positions – and now we begin to get some small hint of what Marx is presenting – are associated here with political economy. They do not reflect Marx's own analyses, but analyses he has set out to criticize.

Marx now launches into a convoluted and implausible series of dialectical analyses of the commodity form. At first glance, it could appear that we have now reached Marx's method of inquiry: Marx may begin with taunting parodies of empiricist and transcendental analyses, but now that the dialectics has begun, surely we have reached his analysis proper.

If so, we should hold some severe reservations about Marx's materialist *bona fides*. The third section of *Capital*'s opening chapter presents us with an idealist dialectic: it identifies a series of 'defects' in categories derived from the commodity form; each defect drives toward a more adequate category, until finally the argument announces that we now understand the origins of money.[75] Read at face value, the passage strongly implies that the logical deficiencies of a set of conceptual categories resolve themselves by compelling the manifestation of a real sociological phenomenon: money exists, according to the logic of this section, because without it the concept of the commodity would be defective.

This section is shot through with gestures that suggest that Marx is deeply amused by this presentation. Sarcastic footnotes, ludicrous analogies, and sardonic asides strongly suggest that these passages are not meant to be taken literally. Francis Wheen has memorably described this section as a 'picaresque journey through the higher realms of nonsense', in which the reader is confronted with increasingly surreal meditations on the interactions of the linen and the coat, until finally driven to realize that the whole presentation is, in Wheen's words, 'a shaggy dog story'.[76] More analytically, Dominic LaCapra has argued that this section is best read as a series of dominant and counter-voices, with the effect of undermining the reader's identification with the overt argument:

> Bizarre footnotes on Benjamin Franklin and on the problem of human identity appear to cast an ironic light on the concept of abstract labor power as the essence or 'quiddity' of exchange values. An ironic countervoice even surfaces in the principal text to strike dissonant notes with respect to the seemingly dominant positivistic voice. ('The fact that [linen] is [exchange] value, is made manifest by its equality with the coat, just as the sheep's nature of a Christian is shown in his resemblance to the Lamb of God.') The reader begins to wonder whether he should take the concepts of abstract labor power and exchange value altogether at face value.[77]

The sarcastic tone of much of the section operates to distance the reader from the dialectical analysis of the wealth of capitalist societies, differentiating this presentation from Marx's own method of inquiry.

Even for Marx, however, sarcasm eventually reaches its limits. This section of *Capital* also includes a moment where Marx finally breaks the fourth wall and provides some more explicit guidance on his own analytical approach. He does this in the form of a mischievous digression on Aristotle.[78]

Prior to this digression, the text has displayed a series of analyses of the wealth of capitalist society, each of which operates as though decontextualized thought were sufficient to achieve sociological insight. The initial, empiricist, analysis of the wealth of capitalist societies suggested that one had only to observe the self-evident properties of the commodity, understood as a straightforward given – as data. The second, transcendental, analysis suggested that empirical observation might not be enough: the commodity also possesses properties that are not immediately perceptible by the senses. Fortunately, these properties can be logically intuited by reason. The third, dialectical, analysis suggested that commodities could not be understood in their static isolation – that a dynamic dialectical analysis is required to grasp how commodities develop in interaction with other commodities. For all their differences, these approaches share the presupposition that the mind's brute force can penetrate all obstacles to arrive at a clear sense of the wealth of capitalist societies.

This presupposition is playfully destabilized when Marx suddenly asks why Aristotle was not able to deduce the existence of value.

This seemingly innocent question carries devastating implications. If the brute force of thought were all that were required to deduce value and to analyze its properties, then surely Aristotle would have been bright enough to deduce it. Indeed Aristotle is bright enough – Marx helpfully points out – to consider the possibility that something like value might exist. Nevertheless, he rejects it out of hand. But why?

What Aristotle lacked, Marx goes on to argue, was not intellect or brute logical force. It was a particular kind of practical experience:

> Aristotle was unable to extract this fact, that, in the form of commodity-values, all labor is expressed as equal human labor and therefore as labor of equal quality, by inspection from the form of value, because Greek society was founded on the labor of slaves, hence had as its natural basis the inequality of men and of their labor-powers. The secret of the expression of value, namely the equality and equivalence of all kinds of labor because and in so far as they are human labor in general, could not be deciphered until

the concept of human equality had already acquired the permanence of a fixed popular opinion. This however becomes possible only in a society where the commodity-form is the universal form of the product of labor, hence the dominant social relation is the relation between men as possessors of commodities. Aristotle's genius is displayed precisely by his discovery of a relation of equality in the value-expression of commodities. Only the historical limitation inherent in the society in which he lived prevented him from finding out what 'in reality' this relation of equality consisted of.[79]

This explanation ricochets back on everything that came before. If a specific kind of practical experience is required, in order for certain 'logical' conclusions to be drawn, or observations made, then the forms of analysis prominently displayed so far in this chapter have not grasped why they are able to arrive at the conclusions they do. An adequate analysis would expose the relationship between practice and thought. Nothing that we have seen thus far in *Capital*'s opening chapter attempts this feat. We have instead been reading an exemplary presentation of several competing forms of analysis that Marx has caricatured in this chapter as the opening volley of his critique.

We have been given our first clear hint about Marx's actual method of inquiry: that he seeks to explain the practical experiences that prime specific sorts of perception and cognition. We have also been given our first clear hint about what is being presented here: competing forms of theory that fail to recognize their own entanglement in determinate sorts of practical experience. Over the course of *Capital*, Marx will develop these hints, recurrently putting on display competing forms of theory, gradually connecting each one with the sort of practical experience that renders that theory socially valid – but only for a bounded slice of social experience. To the extent that a particular kind of theory remains unaware of its current sphere of social validity, and thus over-extrapolates and hypostatizes a narrow slice of social experience to the exclusion of others, that theory can be convicted for expressing a partial and one-sided conception of capitalist society.

One of Marx's goals, then, is to demonstrate the partial and one-sided character of competing theories of capitalist production. His analysis operates by demonstrating the narrow boundaries within which specific theoretical claims can be said to be valid, and then by panning back from those boundaries to show other dimensions of capitalist production, which render valid very different sorts of claims. In this way, Marx gradually explores the internal variability of capitalist production, and mines a much wider array of social experience than do competing forms of theory.

The breadth of his analysis is related to its critical power: by grasping the reproduction of capital as a much more internally diverse and multifaceted phenomenon than competing theories, he renders capitalist history citable in more of its moments. He is positioned to grasp, not simply the end result – the replication of a set of aggregate historical trends characteristic of capitalist production – but also the contradictory countercurrents that imply possibilities for the development of new forms of collective life. By systematically cataloguing each aspect of the complex process by which capital is reproduced – by refusing to reductively equate capitalist production with a small set of aggregate results of this process as a whole – Marx seeks to bring the internal variability of capitalist production squarely into view.

Post Festum Knowledge

Why not declare that this is the intent? Why not explain the presentational strategy and state the actual analytical method overtly?

In part, no doubt, the explanation is that Marx did not anticipate how obscure his readers would find his presentational strategy. Marx viewed the discourse of political economy as self-evidently absurd – its categories as 'deranged' – and he expected his readers to share his sense that these categories could be socially valid only for an irrational form of production. More problematically, he seems to have taken for granted that his readers would then understand that a burlesque style of presentation would be required to adequately express the absurdity of this system. He did not foresee how many readers would approach the text 'straight'.

In part, however, Marx attempted to write the text in a way that exemplified his own understanding of the interdependence of thought and everyday social practice. In the fourth section of *Capital*'s opening chapter, in a passage that is seemingly specific to political economy's discovery of the lawlike patterns generated by capitalist production, Marx describes how knowledge arises after the fact, as we are confronted with the consequences and implications of what we collectively do:

> Reflection on the forms of human life, hence also scientific analysis of those forms, takes a course directly opposite to their real development. Reflection begins *post festum*, and therefore with the results of the process of development already to hand.[80]

This passage is neither an offhand description of the method of political economy, nor a general claim about human knowledge as such: instead, it represents an accidental historical insight that lies ready to hand due to the peculiar characteristics of capitalist production.[81] Once constituted by this accident of history, however, this insight is available to be appropriated and redeployed in a new form – in this case, as one of the cornerstones of *Capital*'s presentational strategy.

Consistently through the text, Marx will mobilize this *post festum* structure. The text will first enact a phenomenon and then – sometimes many chapters later – Marx will make explicit what that phenomenon implied, and explore how it can be appropriated. The text embodies its own claim that first we act, blindly and without a clear sense of the full implications and consequences of our actions – generating possibilities in a state of distraction. Once we have acted, we can then reflect consciously on our actions, tease out their implications – and become able to re-enact and creatively adapt our insights to novel ends.

Marx thus treats *Capital* as a *production* – and flags this in the opening chapter by treating the main text as a stage, onto which he casts actors who represent common approaches to theorizing the wealth of capitalist societies. Only after actually staging this play does he then – in chapter 2 – explicitly tell his readers that his investigation proceeds by exploring a series of 'characters who appear on the economic stage'.[82] The explicit articulation takes place only *after* the practical enactment – first we act, then we appropriate insights from that enactment – and, in the process, we can transform our relationship to the original act, innovating around and adapting the original performance.

In much later chapters, Marx attaches explicit identities to the original actors. The empiricist figure who opens the chapter is associated with vulgar political economy,[83] while the transcendental figure is associated with classical political economy.[84] The 'social forms' introduced in the original play are gradually revealed to be, not 'elementary forms' from which other aspects of capitalist society can be derived, but rather aggregate results of a vast array of concrete practices that Marx systematically catalogues through the remainder of the volume.[85]

In each successive chapter, Marx makes explicit further implications of the practices and forms of theory articulated in previous chapters. Readers who do not recognize that this strategy is in play will commonly miss the strategic point of long passages of text – particularly early in the work, when less has been enacted, and little can be stated explicitly.

Many important implications of the social practices that reproduce capital are simply not visible from the standpoint of a single practice, or even a collection of several dozen practices. This is precisely why so many forms of theory derive such inadequate conceptions of capitalist production: they are focusing on too narrow a slice of social experience. Thus, for example, when Marx first introduces the category of capital in chapter 4, he has already explored dozens of different social practices. This exploration enables him to *introduce* the category – but only as it appears from the standpoint of those social practices associated with the circulation of goods on the market.

As it happens, when viewed from the standpoint of circulation, capital appears to be a self-organizing, autonomous entity, unbounded by material constraints. It appears, in other words, rather like it does to the political economists: as a spontaneously self-organizing system.

Marx distances himself from this interpretation with a heavy dose of sarcasm. He deploys Hegelian vocabulary to draw out the idealist mystification of this perspective, describing capital as a self-moving subject that is also substance – attributing to capital, in other words, the qualities of Hegel's *Geist*.[86] Marx expects his readers to regard this image as self-evidently absurd but, just in case the reference is too obscure, he also compares this image of capital to the Christian Trinity[87] and to the fairy tale of the goose that lays the golden eggs.[88] This chapter presents, in other words, an infantile fantasy conception of capital as a *sui generis* phenomenon that spontaneously brings forth wealth from itself, unbounded and unrestrained. It does not outline Marx's own conception of capital, but his mocking, sardonic critique of a set of blinkered economic theories and philosophies that mobilize only the smallest fraction of the insights that could be mined from the analysis of capitalist production, and thus remain awestruck by a phenomenon they only dimly understand. This is the description of capital as it appears from the standpoint of circulation.

The phenomenon will appear very different once Marx can mobilize the insights available in other dimensions of social experience.

To articulate a more adequate understanding of capital, Marx must move past the sphere of circulation – into analyses of the sphere of production, the state, and the world system. He will only explicitly articulate his own conclusions, however, once he has explored *all* of the practical actions required to generate a particular social insight. Until then, sarcasm is his principal tool for flagging his personal distance from the perspectives explored in his main text.

Since text is necessarily linear, and not every practice can be explored simultaneously, the result is often that Marx must string together many chapters before he has assembled the insights needed to articulate important conclusions. By the time he can render the analysis explicit, the reader has often forgotten the many earlier passages in which he painstakingly assembled the diverse building blocks on which specific conclusions rely. Marx's conclusions can thus seem ungrounded and obscure – dogmatic assertions, instead of carefully substantiated arguments. By the same token, long sections of text can appear not to make any substantive contributions to the overarching argument – and are thus often not discussed, or even edited out!, by interpreters keen to zero in on what they take to be the heart of the argument.[89] But these long, detailed passages are where Marx carries out the heart of his analysis – where he outlines capital's 'microscopic anatomy'.

Microscopic Anatomy

In this short piece I cannot adequately explore how this microscopic anatomy plays out. I can, however, indicate what *sort* of analysis Marx is making – and explain how this analysis overcomes the subject/object divide in a very different way to that assumed by contemporary theories of social form.

122

In chapters 2 and 3 of *Capital*, Marx starts to explore a series of micrological social practices. He does this in excruciating detail, and with no explicit indication of what strategic purpose the analysis serves. He begins with practices associated with a petty bourgeois experience of capitalist production – practices that could all conceivably be undertaken by persons who produce goods using their own personal labor, bring these goods to market, and exchange them for other goods that they personally need.

Along the way, Marx highlights the material result of this process – the exchange of material good for material good. This material result is a real aspect of contemporary capitalist production: we really do move goods from one place to another, engaging in what Marx calls a process of 'social metabolism'.[90] This real result, however, tells us nothing about the process through which the result has been achieved. The same material result would arise from direct barter, or from a customary process of the exchange of goods. If we focus entirely on the result, we will arrive at a very partial and one-sided understanding of the process.

At the same time, the material result cannot be disregarded. It generates real effects, which form part of the real internal variability of capitalist production. These real effects suggest specific possibilities for future social development – including some possibilities that would carry social development in directions that are not compatible with the continued reproduction of capital. In this sense, these real effects enable practical experiences that can be mobilized critically, to advocate alternative forms of collective life.

Some contemporary theorists have picked up on one possible emancipatory implication of this particular real effect, and have argued that Marx intends to advocate for a form of collective life in which social wealth is based on material wealth, rather than on value.[91] While this may indeed be an important potential, Marx's actual understanding of emancipatory possibilities is much more complex, mining many different dimensions of the internal variability in the practices that reproduce capital. The end result is a rich and complex network of emancipatory resources that Marx catalogues throughout his text.

Having explored the implications of the material result, Marx pans back to look at the same phenomenon from a broader perspective – that of the process by which this material result has been achieved.[92] By panning back in this way, Marx can criticize as one-sided and partial any forms of theory that over-extrapolate from this small aspect of capitalist production. He can also begin assembling the resources to make a *prima facie* case that capitalist production itself suggests the possibility for alternative means to achieve this same result – thus refuting charges that his critique is utopian or impractical given current levels of technological sophistication or complexity of the division of labor.

This basic process will continue through the whole length of *Capital*. In each new section, Marx will systematically catalogue dimensions of social experience, point out which competing forms of theory fixate on the dimension just analyzed, ask what other social purposes could be pursued when deploying the same sorts of social actions, and then pan back to look at capitalist production from a different perspective.

But what does all this have to do with the subject/object divide?

When carrying out his microscopic anatomy, Marx stages a series of miniature plays. He is analyzing micrological social practices, and to do so he seeks to capture, not just what sorts of impacts people create in the external world, or what sorts of interactions they carry out with other people, but what sorts of bodily comportments, strategic orientations, forms of perception and thought, and other subjective states are part and parcel of a specific social performance. The narrative form of the play allows Marx to capture the subjective, intersubjective and objective elements of each social practice that he explores. It also allows him to thematize how what is superficially the 'same' act, carried out with the same prop and on the same stage, might nevertheless be part of a very different performance, depending on the subjective orientations, intersubjective relations, or objective impacts enacted.

Thus, for example, the common prop we call 'money' can be variously used by buyers and sellers, debtors and creditors, thieves and heirs, bankers and governments, and a wide cast of other characters who enact different sorts of performances facilitated by this same basic prop. These performances, however, constitute different sorts of subjective stances, intersubjective relations, and objective consequences – they generate different immediate consequences, and different potentials for current and future social development. Unless this diversity is recognized, theorists may conflate fundamentally different kinds of social performance, overlook contradictory social trends, and fail to grasp important potentials for alternative forms of collective life. The theatrical narrative style of Marx's work is designed to maximize his ability to keep track of the performative diversity that can differentiate superficially similar kinds of social practices. It enables Marx to map several different dimensions of social practices simultaneously, in a way that clearly demarcates and preserves social diversity.

This approach allows Marx to relate social forms of subjectivity and objectivity to one another, not because these forms all share the same fractal structure, but because determinate subjective stances, intersubjective relations, and objective consequences are always part and parcel of any given social practice. For this reason, Marx does not end up pointing all social performances back to a small number of social forms that purportedly permeate social interaction. Instead, he ends up cataloguing dozens and dozens of differentiated types of performances, each integral to the reproduction of capital, but each also generating their own distinctive consequences and potentials when considered in isolation or when grouped together with a subset of the other practices required for capitalist production.

Many of the performances Marx traces are fleeting and ephemeral moments embedded in longer chains of related practices. We enact many of these performances in a state of distraction, while focusing on more overarching goals. And yet these fleeting practical experiences, which may fly beneath the radar of ordinary awareness, nevertheless provide a reservoir of experience that can be mined and rendered explicit for emancipatory ends. The experience of human equality figures as one of these fleeting moments – contradicted by many more prominent aspects of social experience, so that the conviction that humans are equal emerges initially, in Marx's words, as a 'fixed popular opinion'[93] – something we intuitively feel is correct, but whose origins we have difficulty tracing, because we enact a peculiar kind of equality accidentally, in the course of a performance that has very different overt goals. Once enacted, however, human equality becomes a particularly important component of the reservoir of practical experience that can be wielded for emancipatory ends.

Selective Inheritance

How does all this relate to the question with which I opened – the question of how Marx understands the immanent generation of emancipatory potential? A seemingly throwaway line in *Capital's* opening chapter provides an important hint. Ostensibly speaking about 'production' in a narrow economic sense, Marx argues: 'When man engages in production, he can only proceed as nature does herself, i.e. he can only change the form of the materials.'[94] I suggest that Marx understands this principle also to apply to our production of human history. For Marx, emancipatory potentials are not created *ex nihilo*, through some sort of abstract leap outside history. Instead, they are appropriated – seized from the circumstances in which they originated, repurposed, and institutionalized anew. Once again, the spirit of the argument is Darwinian: although there is no *telos* driving historical development in a particular direction, later forms of social life are descended, with modification, from earlier forms. Moreover, the development of new forms of social life does not take place in a completely random way. It is mediated by an opportunistic process of selective inheritance that draws upon the pre-existing variability present in the original society in adapting to a changing historical environment.

Within this framework, Marx's microscopic anatomy serves two crucial purposes. First, it shows how an extremely diverse array of micrological social practices could unintentionally generate the sorts of social forms described in *Capital*'s opening chapter – how order could arise without the need for a mystical designer. Second, it demonstrates how inadequate it would be, to reduce our social experience to the set of aggregate patterns that are captured by these social forms. These patterns are *part* of the internal variability of capitalist production – a particularly striking and, for political economy at least, awe-inducing part, which requires for its generation the tandem operation of all of the social practices Marx catalogues in *Capital*. Yet the same practices that operate together to generate such aggregate effects, also generate effects at much more local scales, which do not require the continued operation of the system as a whole, and which suggest alternative ways of institutionalizing the aspects of capitalist production we might want to preserve.

Capital's critical standpoint relies on keeping firmly in view this vast reservoir of internal social variability. It refuses to look *through* this complex, chaotic content, in order to reductively grasp capitalism as a system defined only by the reproduction of a small set of social forms. Instead, it sees the reproduction of capital as dependent on a vast assemblage of social practices that possesses high internal variability. Through a process of selective inheritance, it is possible to mobilize this internal variability, adaptively improvising new forms of collective life. Communism would be capitalism, some disassembly required: a speciation from our existing form of social life, which would creatively adapt existing social potentials to emancipatory ends.

6

Work, Work Your Thoughts, and Therein See a Siege
Anthony Iles and Marina Vishmidt

Art's double character as both autonomous and fait social is
incessantly reproduced on the level of its autonomy.
Theodor Adorno

If you take hold of a samovar by its stubby legs, you can use
it to pound nails, but that is not its primary function.
Viktor Shklovsky

Introduction

Recent moves in political aesthetics have posited a communist moment in
so-called 'relational art' through which experiments in collectivity and con-
viviality outline a potential post-capitalist praxis to come.[95] The recent up-
take of the post-autonomist immaterial labor thesis draws cultural practitioners closer to the critical self-recognition of their own labor (waged and
otherwise) as alienated, as well its formal commonality with other kinds of
affective labor at large. Art finds itself in a new relation with contemporary
forms of value production. This applies also to the structural re-composi-
tion of work in the image of the 'creative' and self-propelled exploitation

typical of financialized capitalism. In an unprecedented way, art not only reflects but revises the productive forces, shading into forces of 'non-production' and devalorization in an era of debt-financed austerity. However, as art expands to include more and more fields of social action within its imaginative and institutional remit (political activity, work, education), the paradox remains that the social effectiveness of art is guaranteed by its separation from capitalist work. Thus, art's estrangement from labor continues apace, but, at this historical juncture, coincides with labor's estrangement from labor: laboring subjects who do not identify with themselves as labor. On the one hand all labor becomes in some sense aesthetic self-creation, on the other, formerly unalienated activities are subsumed by capitalist social relations as never before.

In this text, we will discuss the complex through which art and culture register and inscribe social relations of production as they develop from the struggles between capital and labor, examining points of convergence and divergence with the communization thesis.

Communization

Central to communization theory is the premise that the chief product of the capitalist mode of production is the class relation between capital and labor. This social relation is evidently breaking down in the West as de-valorization and debt replaces expansion in financialized economies. At the same time, it can be argued that the spread of market relations in China and Southeast Asia is eclipsed by the global growth of populations that are surplus to the requirements of accumulation.[96] Observing capital's victories through thirty years of neoliberal restructuring, communization theory contends that the self-affirmation of the working class is not only defunct as a political strategy, but was historically at the core of its defeat. This stemmed from a failure to attack the category of value. Value, with its twin poles of use-value and exchange-value, is the real abstraction that mediates all social relations through the commodity. Communization would be the realisation of the human community through the destruction of the value-form, not a mere takeover of existing means of production.[97]

> Revolution previously, [...] was either a question of workers seizing the productive apparatus from this parasitic class and of destroying its State in order to rebuild another, led by the party as the bearer of consciousness, or else of undermining the power of the bourgeois State by organising production themselves from the bottom up, through the organ of the trade unions or councils. But there was never a question or an attempt of abolishing the law of value...[98]

By contrast to this tradition, described by Théorie Communiste (TC) as 'programmatism', communization poses the question of why and how communism is possible now when the class relation which reproduces capital is breaking down. The development of capital progressively empties work of content as it strives toward real subsumption.[99] Class and labor are experienced as an 'external constraint', they can provide neither perspective nor legitimacy to current struggles, which encounter them as a limit. Endnotes discuss the redundancy of the wage in today's capitalism: 'As the wage form loses its centrality in mediating social reproduction, capitalist production itself appears increasingly superfluous to the proletariat: it is that which makes us proletarians, and then abandons us here.'[100]

It is possible to draw a link between the critique of labor as a ground for human emancipation (communism) in the communization account and the critique of labor found in critical aesthetics, from Schiller onwards, which proposes a genuinely human community bonded together by play rather than production; collective self-determination as a work of art. The idea of an immediate appropriation of the world, of determinate negation of what is, in some ways evokes an aesthetic rather than a political view of the content of revolution. The affirmation of direct social relations unmediated by the alienating abstractions of money, state or labor is an invariant across Romantic aesthetics and is reflected in utopian socialist theory preceding Marx's work. Thus, we can begin to see an aesthetic dimension to communization.

The Utopia of Exact Living

Our departure point is that there is both an analogy and a disjunction between the premise of ultra-left communism, specifically communization, and the premise of many radical art practices. The project of the dissolution of art into life – expressed variously in surrealism, the situationists, Dadaism, constructivism, productivism, futurism, conceptual and performance art – has drawn life into art's orbit but also bound art closely to the potential transformation of general social life. The analogy is that communism argues for the generalization of creativity through the overcoming of the social domination of abstract labor and the value-form, which also means the dissolution of the boundary between a reified creativity and a rarefied uselessness – art – and the production of use-values – work.

The disjunction, on the other hand, comes from the tradition of critical Marxist aesthetics, which argues that it is precisely the other way around – art must maintain its difference from capitalist life in order to exert a critical purchase on it. It is the degree to which the separation between art and life, between art and work, is viewed as a problem which can be overcome in the here and now or the symptom of a problem which only social revolution can address that marks the difference between these two traditions. Fundamentally, they are premised upon different ideas of art's role in capitalist subsumption. Would art disappear in communism or would everything become art? The same question can be asked about work – would communism entail a generalization or the abolition of work? After 500 years of capitalism, are we any longer in a position to distinguish the capitalist forms from the unadulterated contents, i.e. work and capitalist work, art and commodity art, life and capitalist life?

Frames of Struggle

Artists on the Assembly Line

If art's emancipatory qualities are founded upon the tensions between self-directed activity and productive labor then attempts to close the distance between them are of paramount importance. The early 20th century avant-garde saw many such attempts. The artist going into industry has always had an element of dressing up, just as communist intellectuals in Weimar Germany competed, both in their lives and their works, to 'look' more pro-letarian. Rodchenko dressed in a 'production suit' continues to haunt left historians and artists. The most radical Soviet constructivist and produc-tivist artists appear to be participating in a dress rehearsal for a putative revolutionary role curtailed by Stalinism. The irony is that if artists had completely dissolved themselves into the figure of the worker we would know no more of them.

Yet, this narrative, of a true avant-garde defeated by Stalinism and the NEP (New Economic Policy), has been transformed in recent years. Maria Gough's research on the factory placement of constructivist Karl Ioganson shows that interventions by constructivist artists in industrial production did in fact take place during the NEP.[101] The debates between constructivist and productivist tendencies within INKhUK (the Soviet 'Institute of Artistic Culture', 1920-26) about how to close the gap be-tween productive and aesthetic labor are also instructive. From these, John Roberts isolates three potential roles for the artist intervening directly in the production process: the artist as an engineer contributing to the im-provement of industrial technique, the artist as designer establishing new product lines, and lastly the artist as a catalyst or spiritual engineer seeking 'to transform the consciousness of production itself in order to contribute to labor's emancipation'.[102]

The practical experiments in the production process by con-structivist artists fulfilled only the first and second of these roles. With the adoption of rationalising Taylorism as Bolshevik policy in the rapid industrialisation during NEP, Soviet production did not depart from, but rather aped value-production (albeit in a dysfunctional form). Progress was regression. Effectively artists worked to discipline and police workers in the work place and outside it. Yet, if for Roberts the third position remains a utopian horizon then this leads to many questions. In a collaboration between artists and workers, what makes the artist the catalyst in transforming the production process? And, more importantly, is this 'emancipation' *from* labor or *as* labor?

A proponent of 'left' productivism, Boris Arvatov, made a contribution to this debate which was overlooked at the time and only recently recovered. His theoretical output attempts to close the distinction between production and consumption enforced by capital and reproduced intact in most Marxist theory. Arvatov foregrounds the status of *things* as central to the communist transformation of everyday life: 'If the significance of the human relation to the Thing has not been understood, or has been only partially understood as a relation to the means of production, this is because until now Marxists have known only the bourgeois world of things.'[103] Arvatov insists that the polarities which organize bourgeois life would be completely dissolved under communist social relations. Freed from possession as private property, things are also freed from the subject-object relations through which capitalism subordinates human life to the demands of the production process and thus capital's own valorization process.

Arvatov hardly mentions art in this important essay, but remains primarily a theorist of the artistic trends associated with constructivism. His prefiguration of a 'communist object' and new materialist social relations sits uneasily with art and labor's instrumentalization under Bolshevism. Notwithstanding a technocratic outlook and a problematic affirmation of labor (albeit labor redefined under socialist conditions), Arvatov's ideas hold out significant opportunity for development. He allows us to jettison the crude Marxian idea that science and technology are neutral means to be appropriated by the proletariat and enables us to pose the problem of communism as not only a change in ownership, but a total departure from the capitalist mode of production and its 'scientific' foundation. A transformation of ontological oppositions: production and consumption, everyday life and labor, subject and object, active and passive, exchange-value and use-value. Drawing upon the insights of Walter Benjamin on collecting, we can speculate that it is only things liberated from use which cease to be commodities. The socialist object is not just one that's been taken out of commodity exchange and put to good use in a new society; if it was really socialist, it would never be put to use as we know it.[104]

The Communist Imaginary

In his writing on relational aesthetics and socially-engaged art practices John Roberts notes a disconnect between such practices and a critique of work.[105] Roberts sees in this activity a valuable 'holding operation' which 'keeps open the ideal horizon of egalitarianism, equality and free exchange.' Stewart Martin disagrees: 'The dissolution of art into life not only presents new content for commodification, but a new form of it in so far as art or culture has become a key medium through which commodification has been extended to what previously seemed beyond the economy'.[106] Recent accounts of the relation between productive labor and artistic labor refer to post-autonomist ideas of the socialisation of work in advanced capitalism. Central to these accounts is Maurizio Lazzarato's concept of 'immaterial labor' – the notion that all work is becoming increasingly technologized, dependent upon and productive of communication and cooperation rather than a finished product.

However, almost immediately after its formulation Lazzarato abandoned the term:

> But the concept of immaterial labor was filled with ambiguities. Shortly after writing those articles I decided to abandon the idea and haven't used it since. One of the ambiguities it created had to

do with the concept of immateriality. Distinguishing between the material and the immaterial was a theoretical complication we were never able to resolve.[107]

In the early 21st century claims for the hegemony of a class of immaterial laborers could be disputed by pointing out the drive of capital towards absolute surplus-value extraction in the global south. After the 2008 financial crisis, the dramatic shake out of overinflated values and optimism about the agency of this new class brought to new light the relation between the material and the immaterial. Furthermore viewing contemporary labor through the lens of immaterial labor tended to reproduce rather than disassemble the dominant division of mental and manual labor in capitalism. Art as such can be seen as the fetishization of the division of mental and manual labor, which is refined and generalised in the 'creativization' of 'post-Fordist' work.

An interesting way out of the sterility of such debates, is identified by Stewart Martin in his essay 'The Pedagogy of Human Capital', in which he discusses how terminology such as immaterial labor and self-valorization both operate with a problematic concept of autonomy. Autonomy can be said to have been thoroughly internalised by capital in its attempts to collapse the subjectivity of living labor as its own and through its moves to commodify previously non-capitalised areas of life. The move to aesthetics is then seen as a way of dissolving the autonomy/heteronomy distinction, reliant ultimately on domination (even and especially when it's the 'self-legislating' kind), through the agency of play and the invention of 'forms-of-life' resistant to an autonomy thinkable only through capital's laws.[108]

What is There in Uselessness to Cause You Distress?

In art from the 1960s onwards late capitalist modernity offered some exits for practitioners who saw the division of labor between art work and regular work as a political issue. There was a 'refusal of work' within art, rejecting art making and socialisation as an artist by exiting the art world and becoming invisible or imperceptible on its terms. There was also the emulation of work in the art domain, from proletarian stylistics to managerial protocols, marking the shift to the 'post-industrial' era in the West. Feminism's influence was seen in practices which problematized the division of art work from domestic labor. Conceptual art itself was premised on an expansion of art's competence via the dissolution of its borders. The paradoxical identification with extra-artistic labor while rejecting artistic labor entered another phase with artists such as Gustav Metzger (leader of an art strike and proponent of auto-destructive art) and the Artist Placement Group.

The Artist Placement Group, operating in the UK and Europe from 1966–1989, was started by John Latham, Barbara Steveni and others. Their central concept was 'placing' artists in organizations, a forerunner to artist residencies. The main differences with the artist residency as it exists now was that the artist was re-defined as an Incidental Person, a kind of disinterested and de-specialised agent who might prompt a shift in the context into which he or she was inserted, promising no specific outcome beyond that. The maneuvers of repudiation of art, whether it was negative, e.g. withdrawal from art, or positive, e.g. expansion of art's remit, were subjected to a 'knight's move' by APG, whose idea of the Incidental Person (IP) managed to at once de-value art and de-value work. It bracketed both 'art' and 'work' in the emergent concept of the 'professional' as a neutral and unmarked social being. It also re-constituted artistic subjectivity at what can be viewed as a higher level of mystification: a valorization of the artist as the place holder for human freedom elsewhere cancelled in capitalist society. This conception is linked to the Romantic aesthetic tradition, and can be found across 19th century philosophers such as Friedrich Schiller and William Hazlitt, as well as authors working in the Marxist critical aesthetics vein, such as Theodor Adorno, pointing to their shared reference to art as unalienated labor.

To give a specifically Marxist valence to the idea of an artistic avant-garde, in her book *Marx's Lost Aesthetic*, Margaret A. Rose speculates that Marx not only developed a Saint-Simonian critique of the feudal nature of industrial capitalism but was also influenced by the Comte de Saint-Simon's ideas about artists in society: 'Artists should also be considered as industrialists, as they are producers in many respects and among them they contribute greatly to the prosperity of our manufacturers by the designs and models with which they furnish the artisans.'[109] In his utopian plan for a future society based upon transformed industrial relations Saint-Simon made room for artists in his '"Chambre d'Invention" at the head of his administrative pyramid with engineers and architects.'[110] As Rose points out, since for Saint-Simon politics was a 'science of production', the role of artists was itself a political role, bound up with the multivalent aspects of art, use and poiesis.[111]

Here we can see prefigured the deployment of artists in industry as promoted and practised by APG. The significance of this precursor is not only that from a certain perspective APG reproduce the role of the artist as part of a problematic managerial vanguard of a new system. Saint-Simon's 'prosperity' is not productive in the capitalist sense but emancipates workers from work to pursue 'enjoyments'. It is this which connects APG back to Marx's 'lost aesthetic' and prompts us to reassess their efforts in line with a critique of the organization of activity and of the senses under the capitalist mode of production.

Traditionally, capitalist modernity excluded art from instrumentality because it was seen as an exception, a free creative practice which was pursued for ends different to economic activity, and untainted by politics. But this can also be re-framed as placing art in service of a 'higher' instrumentality, that of displacing and reconciling bourgeois contradictions.[112] The Adornian complex of art as the absolute commodity captures this. The concept of the IP then could be read as a subversive affirmation of this: putting purposeless purpose to work.

Whereas APG's placements were guided by a characteristically obtuse notion of 'use', artists are inserted into social contexts now precisely because they are deemed useful for executing vague state or corporate goals. Such an outcome is already evident in the history of APG trying to 'sell situations' to UK culture bureaucracies in the 1970s, as they alternately embrace and back off from the entrepreneurial and employment potential occasionally glimpsed by the Arts Council in the 'placements'. APG asserted the aim to 'provide a service to Art, not a service to artists', while the notion of the IP is predicated on a loss of self-evidence of what Art is or even its right to exist, as Adorno put it. The opacity of any benefit in the presence of the IP in organizations is framed by APG as economically productive in the visionary sense today's business climate needs. By the early 1980s, the concept of 'human capital' had begun to circulate in policy circles, and APG's proposals started to make more sense.

The presence of the IP in an organization was meant to overcome the antagonism between workers and management, much as the idea of human capital does. It was a process of making real oppositions ideally obsolete through the mediation of this 'third term'. APG's 'non-technical non-solution' thus exposed them to accusations of having social-democratic illusions. A few implications arise here. One is the IP's repudiation of the productivist legacy of sending artists into the factories and improving the labor process: the IP brief was totally undetermined – APG took artistic alienation from productive life seriously. For the APG, however, if art did have a social use, it was not a use recognisable to anyone, but it did have the power to reveal the contingency of social uses, and propose other ones, albeit within the broadly-defined language game of art. Yet this challenge to use-value and useful labor was beholden to a vision of artistic neutrality which can be seen as readily morphing into the non-specialised but omni-adaptable 'creative' of today.

A powerful retort to APG's attempts to expose commodity production to transformative non-instrumental ends can be derived from the case of one of the companies they targeted for placements: Lucas Aerospace. While APG were unsuccessfully approaching management at the company, the Lucas Aerospace Combine Shop Steward's Committee was countering management-imposed restructuring with their own alternative corporate plan. The plan proposed the reorganization of the company around 'socially useful products and human-centered technologies' developed by the workers themselves. Setting out to address 'the exponential change in the organic composition of capital and the resultant growth of massive structural unemployment' directly, the Committee rejected in practice the division of manual and intellectual work.[113] The plan was developed on company time and in the context of sit-ins and demonstrations to contest restructuring. The 'creativity' of labor was matched by, and in fact conditioned by, the negativity of labor – stopping or slowing-down production.

It is important here to note that by no means was the Lucas Corporate Plan simply an experiment in self-management. The plan posed the problem of the emancipation of labor as a struggle over the content of work and the use-values it produces. Yet this approach strategically included both a rejection of and a compromise with the market.

Something about between nothing and money

The conception of use-value as separable from the commodity is questionable in itself. Yet, this separation is also primary to the debate about whether art does or does not have use-value. The answer to this is decisive for art's critical status in capitalism, as much as for debates about the content of communism.

Karl Marx, in his Appendix to the 1st German edition of *Capital*, Volume 1, 'The Value-Form', makes several statements which clarify what is elsewhere an ambiguous relationship between exchange-value and use-value.

The analysis of the *commodity* has shown that it is something *two-fold*, use-value *and* value. Hence in order for a thing to possess *commodity-form*, it must possess a *twofold form*, the form of a use-value and the form of value ... Relative value-form and equivalent form are moments of the *same expression of value*, which belong to one another and are reciprocally conditioning and inseparable.[114]

Therefore, 'use-value and exchange-value, are distributed *in a polar manner* among the commodities'.[115]

Marx discusses use-values always and already in the context of the commodity. Use-value refers to the natural properties of a commodity. Use-values are realised only in consumption, not exchange. A commodity is the crystallisation of social labor, which is performed in a certain configuration of social relations of production. Therefore, we can say that use-value is always mediated by those social relations: 'Use-value is the immediate physical entity in which a definite economic relationship – exchange-value – is expressed'.[116]

While it is accurate to say that use-value exists outside its particular social form, it is the division of commodities into a use-value and an exchange-value that bespeaks the operation of the social form of value. Because all capitalist commodities are products of abstract labor, the dimension of use-value supposedly unrelated to social form is subsumed in this homogeneity and abstraction insofar as use-value is part of the commodity. Use-value bears the same relation to exchange-value as concrete labor does to abstract labor; it is its opposite (particular, individual), but subsumed into the general form of value which hollows out particularity. The fact that (most) art is not produced directly under the law of value does not put it outside the value-form. As such, it might perhaps be more relevant to discuss art in its tenuous link to abstract social labor than simply as anomalous to use-value.

Moishe Postone identifies 'labor' as a capitalist category and thus a reified one.[117] This is relevant also to the de-socialised or idealised positioning of use-value, and ultimately testifies that the art into life versus critical autonomy paradox for art cannot be resolved so long as the social form of its production is determined by value. The form of social labor in capitalism is nowhere the same thing as concrete labor, or even the ahistorical 'metabolic interaction with nature':

> 'Labor' by its very nature is unfree, unhuman, unsocial activity, determined by private property and creating private property. Hence the abolition of private property will become a reality only when it is conceived as the abolition of 'labor' (an abolition which, of course, has become possible only as a result of labor itself, that is to say, has become possible as a result of the material activity of society and which should on no account be conceived as the replacement of one category by another).[118]

This political point is central, i.e. labor cannot serve as a ground for emancipation, which is where Postone crosses over with communization theory in their shared emphasis on value-critique.

Until recently, communist thought posed the problem of production as one of separating use-value from exchange-value, yet these insights suggest that destruction of the capital-labor relationship must also destroy use-value as a constitutive category presupposed by value.

The questions raised by the Lucas Plan are revisited by Bruno Astarian with regard to what he calls 'crisis activity':

> The question is how production can resume without work, or productivity, or exchange. The principle of 'production' without productivity is that people's activity and their relationship come first and output second. To develop production without productivity is

to abolish value in both its forms.[119]

Seen in this light, the Lucas Plan enacts the isolation of a general, and therefore abstract, need (a market as such) and offers production to satisfy it, rather than each producer cooperating to immediately satisfy particular needs. Astarian invokes communization as a form of production inseparable from the particular needs of individuals and in total rejection of measurement and accounting. Particularity and rejection of measurement evokes the aesthetic, here envisioned as not just in reaction to but exceeding the abstraction and value-measure which have prepared the ground for it.

Financialization: Form Follows Finance

We can outline other relationships that bind artworks to the political economy of their times. Theodor Adorno conceives of 'aesthetic forces of production' that inescapably imprint the artwork: 'the artist works as social agent, indifferent to society's own consciousness. He embodies the social forces of production without necessarily being bound by the censorship dictated by the relations of production.'[120] Those relations are legible in art, but encrypted in such a way as to underline their contingency. Jean-Joseph Goux relates Marx's schema of the development of a general equivalent to the invention of forms of representation; of art, literature and language.[121] This system presents modes of signification and modes of exchange as imbricated.

Goux describes capitalist exchange's tendency towards abstraction and the tendency to 'dematerialisation' in art as two sides of a general crisis of representation punctuated by historically locatable crises in the value form (1919, 1929 and 1971). Each crisis marks a limit to the existing system's ability to represent real world goods through money, and in each case resolution of the crisis is by way of an expansion, or further abstraction, of the money-form. Put crudely, the drives towards abstraction in both art and money are entwined.

Art is both an innovator in the forms of representation –
extending the limit of what can be represented – and, at times, its antagonist – eschewing equivalence and disrupting orders of measure.
Art as a special commodity rebels against its commodity status, seeking a transvaluation of all values. 'Great 20th-century avant-garde art
– and poetry in particular – from Celan to Brecht and Montale, has
demonstrated the crisis of experiential units of measure.... This emphasis on immoderation, disproportion [...] is where [avant-garde art]
edges up to communism.'[122] Arguably in the movement towards financialization art has tracked capital's proclivity to escape from engagement with labor and into the self-reflexive abstraction of value. As gold
became paper and then electronic, money increasingly became autonomous from productive labor. The movement of self-expanding value,
appearing as money making money on financial markets, dissolves all
prior values and relationships into abstract wealth. Similarly in art,
expansion of its claims upon material previously alien to it tends towards
the hollowing out of this material's substance. One notable aspect of dematerialisation in art is its temporal coincidence with deindustrialisation
in the late 60s and early 70s. This period saw a re-engagement with industrial materials and (vacant) industrial spaces by artists. Another was the
move towards information systems and new technologies. In this sense,
the conditions set by the movements of finance provide the material and
conceptual parameters for art. Art operates in these conditions but also
upon them to transform their terms. Both speculative commodities, art is
backed by the credibility of the artist and money by the credibility of the
state. Yet art is engaged in an endless testing of its own condition which
anticipates negations of the determinations of the value form from inside,
rather than beyond, its tensions.

If this complicity between money and art has led to unseemly
games with both, the strain of this relationship has also ushered in forms of

critical reflexivity.[123] Throughout art's development in the face of advanced capitalism, tension with commodification gravitates towards uselessness and negation. If, in art we find the outline of an emancipatory practice to come then it is important to bear in mind that this remains a model and not a programme; it is 'a model *of* emancipated labor, not the model through which the emancipation of labor will be accomplished'.[124]

Don't Worry, Mate, It's Only Art, It's Not Worth it, or, the Labor of the Negative

Increasingly, artistic labor apes service work in its performance of affect and civic virtue, whilst capital (at least in the West) appears to be going through an anti-productivist, if not outright destructive turn. Capital's attempts to bind more closely to the market sectors not previously organized according to the law of value – art, but also education – testify to its current problems of valorization, which are affecting the relationship of capital and labor as well as that between art and labor.

The integration of expanses of social experience which used to provide capital with a dialectical contrast and a 'standing reserve' makes itself felt as uselessness and negation in art, in work and in radical politics. It may be ventured that a common tendency of all progressive social movements at the time Goux was writing (1969) was a rejection of labor, even in the labor movements, which fought hard to wrench more money and more life, not more work, from capitalists and the State. Lyotard was writing his famous 'evil' book, *Libidinal Economy* (1974) several years later, arguing that alienated labor is a source of self-destructive jouissance and can never be affirmed as a productive praxis once freed of its value-form integuments. This accords with the communization position – labor, and its class politics, emerge as a hated situation enforced by capital which has nothing to do with emancipation. Given the preceding, it may be said that communization theory, as seen in the texts we have examined by TC, Bruno Astarian or Endnotes, revisits the dialectic between reform or revolution which transfixed the Left in previous eras both as troubled and as seemingly quiescent as this one. However, it transposes that dialectic onto the 'revolution' side to put forward the claim that all previous revolutionary movements were reformist, as they were content to affirm the working class as it is in capital. The necessity of doing otherwise now stems largely from capital's initiative: not only work, but working-class politics, have been made so degraded and irrelevant that no one identifies with them anymore. At the same time, this dis-identification, regardless of the new political articulations that come in its wake, could also be seen as an atomising and decomposing one. The ongoing reproduction of the social relations of capital, with the politics of its class relations shattered, means that competitive individualism becomes the only credible form of human autonomy – and the community of capital the only credible form of the human community. This situation registered quite early in the stronghold of competitive creative individualism that can be said to have prototyped it, that is, art.

This struggle over the wage and struggle against waged work has not been entirely alien to artists who have agitated around the issue of artists' fees. Groups such as W.A.G.E. (Working Artists in the General Economy) demand reimbursement for 'critical value' in 'capitalist value'. This is certainly a materialist critique of the non-reproduction artists are tasked with advancing for everyone – at least they should be paid for it. The barrier to this provocation, which is also implicit to it, is, as Paolo Virno puts it, 'Nowadays artistic labor is turning into wage labor while the problem is, of course, how to liberate human activity in general from the form of wage labor.'[125] This question of liberating human activity is bracketed in the question of artistic labor, which, in its post-object phase, appears as labor which cannot find value on the market, and is thus useless labor, and can only model liberated human activity for free. This shows that art has a problematic relationship to the commodity not only at the level of the artwork, but at the level of labor.

This problem whether applied to labor or a temporality which ultimately comes down to labor-time under the form of value, is not neglected in communization theory, as writers like Bruno Astarian show:

> There is a paradox here: the economic crisis is at its deepest, the proletariat's needs are immense, and the solution is to reject productivism. Indeed, 'production' without productivity is not a production function. It is a form of socialization of people which entails production, but without measuring time or anything else (inputs, number of people, output).[126]

There is a strong temptation to make an analogy between Astarian's 'production without productivity' or 'consumption without necessity' and art's output of 'a product identical with something not produced'. Art stands between a conscious process and an unconscious one, closely tied to the development of individuality and difference. Not only do artworks pass through a moment which bypasses use value, and cannot be subsumed under exchange value, they also connect with a form of activity which presages non-objective relations between subjects, activity which dismantles 'the subject as congealed technology'.[127] Viewed thus communization would be a generalization of art and individuality *different* to that which we live through today.

Conclusion

Marx's ambiguity on use-value can be linked to the ambivalence of the historical artistic avant-garde and left-communism in relation to work. For Adorno, the criticality of art lay in the paradox of autonomy: art was autonomous (free, giving itself its own law) at the same time as it was heteronomous (unfree, imprinted by commodity relations). Presently, we can re-frame this as the tension between a readily-exploited 'creativity' and a withdrawing 'negativity' as the poles, and the pathos, of current art practice. The problem of the historic avant-garde, especially the Soviet example of Productivism, is also the problem of communism – does work need to be valorized or negated, and under what conditions? There has been an ongoing dialectic of art into life versus art against capitalist life. It seems there is a convergence between a certain sort of negationist attitude toward production in art and in certain strands of Marxism. But should the negativity of capitalist value be recognized as well as the negativity of labor-power lest we reify negativity as the simple absence of productivity, anti-politics, futility? Or even a dynamic counter-form – rupture – to the stagnant value-form? To avoid such an easy totalization, the link from art to finance – to self-expanding value, to recursivity and abstraction – has to be maintained. Art's relation to the value-form and role in socialising value-relations emerges in the forming of a speculative subjectivity suited to a speculative economy.

The figure of the Incidental Person denotes a transformation common to both art and labor as social forms. As the artist becomes a template for a generic subjectivity adaptable to all forms of authority and abstraction, work becomes a form lacking identity or outcome. It is the apotheosis of the romantic figure of the artist: 'Art is now the absolute freedom that seeks its end and its foundation in itself, and does not need, substantially, any content, because it can only measure itself against the vertigo caused by its own abyss.'[128] This is the generic subjectivity of the artist, key to Western liberal discourse since the Enlightenment, whether as civic model or as exception that proves the law of capitalist social relations, and it has less relation to the negativity of labor-power than to the negativity of the ever-mutating form of value. Contra to the thesis that the dissolution of the borders between art and productive labor (or art and politics) heralds emancipation, this may be read instead as an index of the real subsumption of generic human capacities into the self-valorization process of a capital which is no longer sure about where value comes from or how to capture it; a process as self-referential and totalising as the expanded field of art.

Strategies of Struggle

7

The Double Barricade and the Glass Floor
Jasper Bernes

1. limit: barrier; bridle: spur

The limits to capital, in Marx's characterisation, are always double, always both constrictive and generative, 'bridle' and 'spur'.[129] Rather than an impediment confronting capital from the outside, these limits *are* capital, are constitutive of capital; capital is 'the living contradiction' because it 'both posits a barrier specific to itself, and on the other side, equally drives over and beyond every barrier.'[130] Elsewhere, Marx distinguishes between these two types of barriers – the one posited, and the one driven over – by using *grenze* (limit, boundary, border) for the first and *schranke* (barrier, obstacle, fetters, constraint) for the second. From the perspective of capital, 'Every limit appears as a barrier to be overcome': capital is a social dynamic which transforms its constitutive bounds into material contradictions, its limits into obstacles, the better to surpass them.

At root, this 'living contradiction' refers to the self-undermining character of the capitalist mode of production: on the one hand, capital posits labor as the source of all value and attempts to absorb as much of it as possible; on the other hand, it employs labor-saving technologies which expunge living labor from production. This is capitalism's primary absurdity and irrationality, since it means that increases in social wealth and productivity tend to appear as unemployment, falling wages, economic stagnation or outright crisis. But we can also observe the dialectic of bridle and spur, limit and barrier, operating in other areas as well. Labor unions, to take one example, function as both a limit on profitability and a means by which capitalist society maintains the consumer purchasing power necessary for the reproduction of profits. The statist regulations of the mid-20th century, in this view, are not so much an external fetters upon accumulation as they are its generative conditions. Eventually, however, they do become a fetter and must be destroyed, as happened in the long period of restructuring beginning in the 1970s.

Though as yet little known, the writers of Théorie Communiste (TC) have produced some of the most poignant writing on the two-fold character of the limit, examining it not only as axiomatic for capital but as the defining condition of the contemporary proletariat. For TC, the proletariat now finds itself confronted with a paradoxical condition where 'acting as a class has become the very limit of class action.'[131] In recent struggles (basically since the mid-1990s) TC note the emergence of new forms of struggle in which 'class belonging [is] an external constraint.'[132] It is no longer possible to propose a politics based upon the affirmation of working-class autonomy, as there is no longer an independent 'workers' identity.' Every affirmation of the class of labor becomes, by necessity, an affirmation of capital: 'in each of its struggles, the proletariat sees how its existence as a class is objectified in the reproduction of capital as something foreign to it.'[133] This is a limit in the double sense above – a fetter on revolutionary action, but also a generative condition which produces the possibility of superseding the capital-labor relationship. The self-abolition of the proletariat is now possible because 'being a class becomes the obstacle which its struggle as a class has to overcome.'[134]

2. glass floor: shattered glass

TC present these ideas in a highly difficult form, and their tracts are written in a dense theoretical shorthand whose esotericism arises, in part, from their placement within a highly specific theoretical milieu (broadly, the French post-ultra-left) defined by equally specific questions and debates.[135] One of the clearest accounts of this dialectic of limits, however, emerges in their essay on the Greek uprising of 2008, *The Glass Floor (Le plancher de verre)*, where the eponymous metaphor of the glass floor serves as a figural elaboration of the limit. The Greek events are 'a theoretical and chronological landmark' because in them a minority fraction of the proletariat put its own class identity into question, attacked it and rendered it visible as an exterior constraint, a barrier.[136] But unlike the moment of the anti-globalization movements and its anonymizing *black blocs*, which TC describe as involving a merely voluntaristic or willed suspension of class identity, in Greece such a suspension took place as a matter of necessity, rather than will, and abandoned with voluntarism all of the sterile claims for 'another world,' all sense of the possibility of constructing an 'alternative.' What we note in Greece is the instantiation of a swerve or gap (*écart*) within the limit:

> To act as a class entails a swerve towards oneself [*agir en tant que classe comporte un écart par rapport à soi*], to the extent that this action entails its own putting into question in relation to itself: the proletariat's negation of its existence as class within its action as class. In the riots in Greece, the proletariat does not demand anything and does not consider itself against capital as the basis for an alternative, it simply does not want to be what it is anymore.[137]

The limit, in this sense, is a positive (or generative) one: it promises the possibility of proletarian self-abolition. But it carries with it a limit in the sense of constraint. Though the Greek uprising marks the advent of a superseded class belonging, it does so in a manner that stands *outside the site of production,* focused instead on the institutions charged with reproducing the class relation (labor unions, social welfare offices); on the market and the commodity (looting and burning of luxury shops); and on the police as a disciplining moment of social-reproduction. Fractions of the working class proper confront capital as circulation or reproduction, as storefront and trade-union office, prison and university, as riot cop and shopping mall. But the point of encounter between capital and labor in the workplace remains quiet: 'By their own practice, they put themselves in question as proletarians in their struggle, but they only did it by separating, in their attacks and in their objectives, the moments and the institutions of social reproduction.'[138] We might take as a particularly illustrative moment here the following resonant sentence in a communiqué issued by 'fellow precarious workers in the occupied ASOEE' (the Athens University of Economics and Business): 'Work during the morning, insurrection at night.'[139] The glass floor, here, appears in diurnal terms, between the day of exploitation and the night of revolts, but it also appears in spatial terms: the occupiers had disrupted or blocked not the economy itself but its ideological manifestation in the school of business, an institution charged with reproducing class relations through the training of managers, entrepreneurs and technocrats.

3. crisis: swerve

Such limits have nothing to do with a failure of will, nor even less with the collapse of various attempts at left-wing hegemony. They originate ultimately in the restructuring of the capital-labor relationship, beginning in the 1970s and, for TC, completed in the mid 1990s. If the post-war period – captioned somewhat unsatisfactorily by the designators 'Fordism' and 'Keynesianism' – saw the subsumption of workers not only as labor power but as purchasing power, 'treated like grown-ups, with a great show of solicitude and politeness, in their new role as consumers,' something else begins to happen during the crisis of the 1970s.[140] The producer-consumer submits to new (and newly repressive) disciplines in the advanced capitalist countries: fragmented and distributed in networks, colonized by rhetorics of self-management and flexibility, rendered part-time and pushed into industries devoted to the sale, distribution, management and circulation of commodities (including labor-power). This reordering of the working class as in-itself – the reordering of what Italian *operaismo* call its technical composition – renders its conversion into the proletariat, as revolutionary self-consciousness, nearly impossible. The restructuring dislocates the working-class from its own self-realization and self-abolition by way of the revolutionary seizure of the means of production.

TC tend to approach the restructuring in formal terms, speaking of an integration of the proletariat within capital – a mutual presupposition of capital and labor – such that any affirmation of a working-class identity is simply an affirmation of capital. The old organs and tropes of working class identity and autonomy – political parties, trade unions, newspapers, meeting halls – have collapsed, and it is no longer possible to propose a dictatorship of the proletariat, a management of the existing forces of production for and by workers.

The relational terms that TC provide are crucial, but we can more fully develop their conclusion about the promises and impasses of the present period by looking at the *material* transformation of capitalism over the last thirty-years, by looking at its technical or use-value side. In advanced capitalist or post-industrial economies, growth has occurred primarily in industries involved with the circulation or realization of commodities (transport and retail); industries designed to manage the reproduction of capital (finance) or labor (education, health care); and finally industries concerned with the administration of flows of goods and bodies (information technology, clerical work, data-processing). Capital depends more and more on erstwhile *unproductive* spheres that accelerate and direct flows of capital and labor from site to site, quickening their turnover and reproduction. The expansion of finance is the central manifestation of this shift, but even the supposedly miraculous effects of information technology seem to have mattered less as a way to increase productivity than as a way to decrease the costs of circulation and administration. Circulation no longer shrouds production in the mystifying forms of false equivalence, but penetrates it, disperses it laterally, and submits it to complex mediations. The 'hidden abode of production' is not so much invisible as inaccessible – covered by a glass floor. And in the 'noisy sphere of circulation' the noises we hear are those of the riot.

The collapse of an autonomous worker's identity is an effect of this fragmentation – there can be no stable standpoint of labor when labor and labor-process itself are broken down into globally-dispersed segments, and then stitched together by a growing pool of proletarianized technical and clerical workers. And since he space of the market, of exchange, is where these fragmented parts come together – where the working-class is itself reassembled, it should come as no surprise that this is where contestation primarily erupts. The blockading of urban flows, the smashing and looting of shops – these tactics are given, in a way, by the material coordinates of the current mode of production.

Overall, the implications of such restructuring are more severe than they may at first seem. Because these complex forms of circulation penetrate the production process at the level of materiality, at the level of use-value – as machinery, infrastructure, built environment – they effectively *presuppose* the market, exchange, or at the very least some form of abstract, impersonal coordination. For anti-state communists, they are a material limit, since we find nowhere, ready-to-hand, the use-values which might form the minimum base of subsistence for a future, decapitalized society. The project of the 'seizure of the means of production' finds itself blocked, or faced with the absurd prospect of collectivizing Wal-Mart or Apple, workplaces so penetrated to their very core by the commodity-form that they solicit nothing less than total destruction. This is different than France in 1871 or even 1968, different than Russia in 1917 or Spain in 1936, places where the industries of the means of subsistence were ready-to-hand and expropriable, where one might have found, in some reasonable radius, the food, clothing, housing and medicine necessary for a future society liberated from the exigencies of value. And yet this barrier is now itself a condition of possibility, since it renders incoherent all attempts to imagine, as past revolutions did, an egalitarian set of social relations laid atop the existing means of production. It is the end of a communist politics that is merely redistributive. If we want communism, then we will have no choice but to take our radicalism to the root, to uproot capital not merely as social form but as material sediment, not merely as relations of production but as productive forces.

These, then, are the limits for communism, limits that we should see as merely the other side of the limits to capital. If it is impossible to project a communist future from present bases, it is also likewise impossible to project a capitalist one. This is because, returning to the point where we began, capital is a self-undermining social dynamic – *the limit to capital is capital itself* – one that establishes by its very own progress forward an increasingly intractable barrier to that progress: by compressing necessary labor (and gaining more surplus labor) it also compresses the pool of workers it can exploit. Since capital must not only reproduce itself but expand, this means that, as the mass of surplus value grows ever larger, it becomes more and more difficult to wring subsequent increases in surplus labor from a relatively shrinking mass of workers. The vanishing of an autonomous 'worker's identity' is not a mere ideological fact, but a real feature of capitalism: the vanishing of workers themselves, of the need for work.

Seen as a totality, capitalism in crisis thus produces masses of labor and masses of capital unable to find each other in the valorization process. This is a periodic phenomenon – crises of this sort recur – but also a linear, tendential one, a problem that becomes more severe as capitalism progresses. It is thus the case that capitalism requires more and more robust institutions capable of forcing capital and labor into encounter, as one forces gasoline and oxygen into a piston, institutions devoted to the reproduction of the capital-labor relationship. Seen in this way, crisis appears not only in the realization of commodities and fictitious capitals – the *salto mortale* from production into the market – but also within the underexamined outside of the capital-labor relationship: the place where one chain of M-C-M´ meets another, where money and commodity capital must fight their way back into the workplace and their rendezvous with labor-power, and where labor-power must be moulded, shaped and forced into the site of production. It is here that private and government financial institutions manipulate the conditions of credit and money supply to induce investment. And it is here, too, that the prisons and universities and welfare-to-work offices discipline labor-power so that the right amount arrives at the right workplace at the right price. The banking crisis, therefore, finds its complement in a university crisis.

Examining capitalism in this way, as a process of production that contains moments both inside and outside of the workplace, allows us to expand our notion of antagonistic agents, to expand our notion of the proletariat – so that it includes the unemployed, students, unwaged houseworkers and prisoners. It also allows us to explain why, over the last few years, university and student struggles are so prominent as recent examples of resistance. Students confront the crisis of reproduction directly, as the cost of job training (tuition) increases, and as the value of such training decreases. Students are a proletariat in formation, denied a middle-class future, indebted like the rest of the working class but indebted before they have begun to even earn a wage full time. They thus exist in a relationship to the formal working class defined by the glass floor.

4. double barricade

Though smaller, relatively, than other anti-austerity campaigns by university students in London or Puerto Rico, the events of 2009-2010 at university campuses in California are some of the most vigorous examples of rebellion in the US in recent years – indeed, they were, until the unfolding events in Wisconsin, probably the only significant resistance to the crisis yet visible in the US. If the glass floor is at present truly the determining condition of class struggle, then we should be able to trace it in this history.

Since these events have been summarized and contextualized in detail elsewhere, I will limit myself to a short recapitulation. As many will know, the state of California is perpetually insolvent, riven as it is by a strong anti-tax conservatism on the one hand and a legacy of liberal social commitments on the other. Because the housing boom and crash and therefore the economic effects of the current crisis have been much stronger in California, California's plight is for the most part simply an accelerated version of the crises affecting other states. The precipitating events for the anti-austerity movement in California were not unique or anomalous but an accelerated version of the status quo in general. In the multi-campus University of California system, this meant fee increases, restructuring of the labor force, reduction in classes and enrolment, the gutting of various programs deemed peripheral, all of which happened at the same as university managers directed their quite ample resources to financial gamesmanship, construction projects, incentive packages, high executive salaries, and the succouring of a bloated and inept administrative layer.

The speed at which these changes came – rendering visible a process of privatization and redefinition of education that remained largely invisible – goes some way in explaining the relative explosiveness of the moment, outpacing the usual political players on campus and escaping the ritual and theatrical forms of protest which had become sedimented into university life. But the sudden radical character of the moment, the appearance here and there of an explicitly communist politics, breaking not only with the representational politics of the existing campus left, but yoking these stances to confrontational, violent tactics, can only be understood by way of looking at the relationship between the university and the larger, post-crisis economic landscape: the crisis rendered visible the 'absent future' of students, as an important text, *Communiqué from an Absent Future*, put it.[141] At the same time as students were being driven from the university, those who would stay, shouldering massive debt loads could not look forward to secure employment in the professional, technical, managerial ranks. Fully half of all new graduates were working jobs – if they had jobs at all – for which a college degree was not necessary. The destruction of the university was taking place alongside a process of proletarianization, in which the proletariat, more and more, was defined not just by exploitation, but by a pure dispossession from even the fact of exploitation. Thus the calls to 'save public education' or reform the university, the calls to restore funding, were met by a much bleaker communist politics that promoted immediate negation and expropriation in the face of an absent future. This is how the glass floor operated – with this radical layer meeting another student layer demanding integration into the system, and both of these layers reflected in the super-exploited campus workers who stood with them on the barricades.

From the very beginning of the university unrest there was significant investment in the idea of a student-worker movement – rather than a simple student movement. But the actual landscape turned out to be more complex than abstract calls for solidarity would make it appear. Although most of the major events involved both work stoppages and student strikes (or walkouts), one can note, primarily in the orientation to *the space of the campus*, an uneasy compound of tactics drawn alternately from the political vernacular of the labor movement on the one hand and student activism on the other. Would we sit *in* or walk *out?* Would we blockade the campus the campus or occupy it? Were we a picket line or a march? There was a crisis of prepositions, if not of verbs, one that originated from the different orientations of different groups to the campus as a space and a material process, with the unions picketing at the entrance to campus, while, somewhat contradictorily, students filled up the space behind them, emptying the buildings and treating the open spaces of the campus according to logics of political assembly and discourse – teach-ins, speak-outs and the like – if not more disruptive tactics like occupation or sabotage. One remained

166

uncertain whether the goal was to shut down the campus by emptying it out or by filling it up, whether the object of attack was a geographical zone or the social relations that took place there, whether the most effective stance took place inside or outside the campus; whether one should over-run every barrier or erect barriers everywhere.

By space, then, I mean less a set of coordinates than a kind of *orientation*, here determined by the different structural positions that different groups occupy with regard to the university's place within the regime of value. The picket line treats the campus as a factory, as workplace, site of production or exploitation, and understands that its geographical encircle-ment negates such production. The 'walkouts' and, later, the occupations of buildings, treat the university as a relay point within the circulation and formation of future labor power, as an apparatus of sorting that reproduces the value of labor-power by including some and excluding others, and that, therefore, legitimates class society through a process of certification and ideological training.

These are by no means clear distinctions – students often work in the university; graduate students, for instance, are both students and workers. These are rather abstractions, positions within the scheme of the university which the actions of individuals animate as material, collective characters. They are real abstractions, but, as with class, any one person might inhabit these positions unevenly. Indeed, given the fact that these positions are in contradiction, they give rise to combinatory orientations that turn out to be defining. From the standpoint of the student much seems to depend on whether one wants to open up *access* to the university and, consequently, future employment opportunities, or whether one sees such employment as already ripped from underneath one's feet.

Most of the student-worker movement remained, it must be said, largely reactive, largely attached to the goal of increasing *access* to the university and therefore incapable of questioning the function of the university with regard to reproduction of capitalist relations. It aimed merely to preserve what was soon to be lost – jobs, education, classes – to *save* or *defend* public education. The preservationist impulse was felt first and foremost in the reluctance of students and faculty to sacrifice class-time to strikes and other disruptions; the preservationists often responded to radical elements with a facile paradox: why shut down the campus to protest the shutting down of the campus? At its limit, the preservationist impulse could convert to a logic of 'transformation' or 'alternatives' – taking over the space of campus, and by extension the task of education, and liberating it – with teach-ins and skill-shares, guerrilla film-screenings, political theatre and the like. This tendency will often speak about *opening up* the space of the university – whether by reducing the onerous fees that exclude poorer students, developing policies and curricula that increase equity or, in its most expansive form, turning over campus property to those who are not part of the 'campus community'.

Alongside the political logic of the opening, one finds, also, familiar figures of closure, negation and refusal – picket lines encircling campus, buildings barricaded, sabotage of university property, small riots – tactics aimed not at transformation but suspension and disruption, tactics that aim to bring the university's activities to a halt, rather than replace them with another set of activities. But the lines between these two forms are not always that precise. We might think that the position of students as quasi-consumers of the use-value of education means that they will exhibit this *preservative* stance, whereas many campus workers, as waged proletarians, might exhibit an indifference to the actual content of their work – seeing it as merely a means to an end and therefore make their struggles about pay and benefits. But the picketers were, except in a very few cases that always involved large contingents of students, rarely willing to physically prevent access to campus, and their withdrawal of their labor was always given, in advance, as merely temporary, a one or at most two-day strike. Given the abysmal record of gains from worker struggles over the last few decades – where even most hard-fought and bitter struggles yield meagre and temporary gains – the willingness of workers to really risk their own jobs in a protracted struggle is low. They, too, for the large part aim to keep existing rights and privileges from being eroded.

Students, then, incline toward a kind of weak positivity – a weak alternativism, replete with dubious rhetorics of democratization and representation. Freed from contestations around the wage, their political imagination becomes more expansive, but often ethereal; workers, on the other hand, fall victim to equally weak forms of refusal, to an enervated *realpolitik*. Students (and I think they act here as stand-ins for a more general 'marginal' figure – the unemployed, the partially employed, all those who are antagonistic to the current order but must fight outside of the point of production) hold a certain latitude of political action; workers a certain consequentiality. And while one might expect airy voluntarism and grim determinism to wear each other down without anything of consequence coming from the face-to-face, what *can* occur in political struggles (and what *did* occur, briefly, in California) is a fruitful mixing of these different impulses or tendencies, where each group recognizes its essential truth in the other. The glass floor, in this respect, is more a hall-of-mirrors in which students meet themselves coming, as workers-in-formation, where workers find, held out for them, their missing antagonism, and where both groups become, in the process, *proletarians*. It is less, as we will see, a figure of division and separation than it is a figure of folding and crossing – in which each group finds itself presupposed, folded into and implicated by the other.

If this is truly the sign under which the contemporary hangs, then any intense manifestation should be legible in these terms. I take as example the dramatic occupation of Wheeler Hall at UC Berkeley on November 20 not only because I know it well – I was there, outside, and can rely on more than written sources – but because its relatively incendiary character provides a strong enough light in which to read the shapes described above, the shape of things to come. The first thing one notices in looking back over the events of the day is the ambiguity of *the barricade* – in other words, the ambiguity of the inside/outside distinction produced above. The barricade is both a police mechanism, an enforcement of the rule of property by the police, and a weapon in the hands of antagonists. While the occupiers barricaded themselves into the second floor of the building – using chairs, u-locks, tie-downs and their own hands to deny the police entry – scores of riot police set up a perimeter around the building, first with police tape and then with metal barricades, which they defended with batons, rubber bullets and the threat of arrest. Then, in a subsequent moment, the police lines were themselves surrounded and briefly overwhelmed by thousands of protesters. The double barricade and the double siege – the occupiers besieged by police themselves besieged– lights up the topology discussed above. As limit, the barricade was both a block against and manifestation of the simplest form of solidarity: physical proximity. As barrier – begging to be overrun – it underscored what those inside the building shared with those outside; it rendered itself impotent and transferred the point of antagonism from the inside to the outside.

We can think of the first moment – the occupation of the building and the locking of its doors – as primarily an act of refusal, an attempt to establish an outside within the administrative regime of the university, its ordering of space and time according to the law of value. But as any number of examples demonstrate, unless the removal of this or that space from the value-form spreads, it becomes quickly reinscribed within such. The police are the agents of this reinscription, but just as often the limits are self-imposed, and the space collapses under its own gravity, leading to bargaining, concessions or a simple lack of will to continue. The outside becomes an inside, and the act of negation converts into this or that form of preservation. To survive, a new outside needs to be set up, new forms of refusal need to take root.

If the earlier topological figure disclosed a division between *those who would turn their back on the university* and *those who would preserve it,* the occupation of Wheeler Hall represents an involution of this topology. The line of demarcation – the picket – converts into the barricades around the building, now on the inside of the campus. The students and workers who gather in front of the police belong to their unbelonging. When they barricade the exits and entrances of the libraries (in order to prevent the occupiers from being brought via tunnels, into other buildings, and from there packed into police vans) they cement their own refusal, disposed spatially both in an outward and an inward direction: theirs is a form of exit that stands in place, a refusal that is also an affirmation. The antagonists on campus have become indistinguishable from the so-called 'outside agitators' – important here and elsewhere – upon whom the university managers blame the unrest. The limits of this or that form of belonging, status or privilege, are for a brief moment shattered by the polarizing force of the barricade. The campus is both truly opened up and, at the same time, closed.

These actions only survive by continuously pushing their own outside in front of them, by opening up spaces of rupture, and continuously inviting and then transcending not only the repression of the police and the rule of property but also forms of settlement, stasis and compromise that can emerge from inside antagonism. Still, against the repressive countermovement of the police, just as important are the alternate forms of belonging or sociality that fill in the space left by the expanding outside. In fact, they *must* fill in this space if the outside continues to grow: the oranges and sandwiches thrown, over the riot-helmeted heads of the police, to the masked occupiers on the second floor window; the cups of soup and energy bars passed out to those assembled in front of the barricades; the spontaneous redecorations of campus; the phone calls and text messages and posts on the internet; the improvised chants. To the extent that, in the space opened up by the rupture, people learn to provide for each other, they fend off the moment of repression.[142] But they can do so only in the context of an expanding rupture, lest they fall back into the idle provision of alternatives that are more of the same.

5. double swerve

Rather lucidly, TC define the central question for a communist theory as follows: 'how can the proletariat, acting strictly as a class of this mode of production, in its contradiction with capital within the capitalist mode of production, abolish classes, and therefore itself, that is to say: produce communism?'[143] The political sequence which they see emerging in Greece and elsewhere suggests that the suspension of proletarian identity which one witnesses on the part of the disenfranchised, futureless youth will migrate into the sites of exploitation proper and the mass of workers will, in realizing the futility of revindicative struggles and self-management both, join with the fraction of rebellious youth. This is the swerve: 'the proletariat's negation of its existence as a class *within its action as a class* [emphasis mine]'; the self-negation heretofore occurring on the margins must move to the center. TC see this swerve as rigorously determined by the structure of the capital-labor relationship, but they still lay a great amount of stress on the agency of workers qua workers. As much as they suggest that there is no longer an affirmable identity for the working class that is not at the same time an affirmation of capital, they still locate the swerve inside the site of valorization, rather than at the point of mutual presupposition between capital and labor, or between the waged and unwaged proletariat. Without denying the necessity of interrupting valorization and value at its source, I wonder if TC do not retain a hint of a certain sentimental workerism, residue of their councilist origins. If the proletariat no longer has a *self* within the site of production, why is it that the swerve of self-abolition must begin there? Why is it not possible for self-abolition – the production of communism – to emerge *in between* the site of exploitation and its outside? And ultimately, what difference does it make if a mode of production based upon value and compulsory labor is abolished from without or within? What difference would it make if the sites of valorization are overtaken by marginal proletarians who have no claim on them or if the workers in those sites communize them, turning them over to come who may? One suspects that communization as such will involve both types of movement, a double swerve, from inside to outside and from outside to inside.

There is a medieval community, a small village on a lord's estate. It's announced by the lord that there is a coming danger – an invading horde, the armies of another estate – that will ruin all of their livelihoods. The lord calls them to arms, to put down their plows and pick up swords, as it were. Those in the community agree that such a threat could ruin them, and even though some recognize the lord's interest is not in their well-being but in the protection of his assets, they get that not fighting will lead to the destruction of their community and resources, individual belongings and things used by all alike. They therefore become militants: that is, not professional soldiers, but coming together as an army of sorts, an exceptional measure to deal with an exceptional threat. And they leave to head off this invasion rather than wait for the battle on their own land. They fight battles, many of them die, but ultimately, the invading army pulls back. When the militants return to their village, they find it in flames. It has been laid to waste by another threat when they were off fighting the battle to which their lord had directed them. Everything is wrecked. At the center of the village, one of the only things that remains standing is the unburnable communal oven, now charred both inside and out. Whether or not the cooking fire within had been kept going seems unimportant.

The topic of this essay is that oven. More than that, it has to do with the connection between that oven as 'common' to its users and that fighting mass as an assembly of those with something 'in common.' It has to do with the mode of relation designated as *common*. We could change the story such that the villagers are not responding to the injunction of a lord to defend but are leaving their world (their everyday circuits, locales, and patterns) to mount an insurrection, to do away with their lord, to make civil war. However, distinct as it seems, it changes little in this case. For the question is: do common things, having things in common, and what is common amongst us have to do with *communism*?

The bigger change is that we are speaking of the social and material relations of capital: there has long been no village to which we might return. As such, the story is both an imprecise allegory for the contradictions of the present and a marker of a mode of life and 'cause' for struggle that seem definitively bygone. Yet there is a tendency, recurring across the spectrum of communist writing, and particularly in positions often seen as aligned to those at stake in this volume, to relate to such a lost commons[144] or 'being in common' in one of three ways:

1

We have lost our commons and our common essence, and communism is the return to what has been left behind: it is an overcoming of the present in the name of this betrayed unity.

2

There are older vestiges of the commons, often material resources such as water, that persist, against capital's attempts to privatize/expropriate/enclose them, and one of our tasks is to defend them. Related argument: capital has generated – or there have generated in spite of capital – new commons, often electronic resources, and one of our tasks is to defend them, 'proliferate' their use, and encourage the spread of the form of the common.

3

The elaboration of communism – the infamous *how* of 'transition,' communization – is a 'making common': acts of sharing, including reappropriation from the ownership of one into the ownership of all (or, in better formations, the ownership of *none*), are the acts that *produce* or *reveal* what is common across singularities.

I do not, as such, disagree with any of these in full.[145] Rather, my targets at hand are:

- the thought of return
- the thought that acts of 'making common,' outside of a scenario of economic and political upheaval, are capable of significantly accelerating a movement toward – or *of* – communism
- the thought that 'the commons' constitute a rupture in the reproduction and circulation of value (that is, that they are disruptive or 'unthinkable' for capital)
- most importantly, the idea that communism has to do with what we have in common with each other

My rejection of these comes from a conviction that communism – the elaboration of capital's contradictions – doesn't begin with what capital hasn't quite gotten around to colonizing. Such a search for pockets, remnants of the past or degraded kernels of the present to be exploded outward, too often becomes a nostalgia, a holding pattern, or, worse, a conception of communism as the project of unfolding a category *of* capital, rather than the development of the contradiction of that category. For capital is a relation, and it is the relation between that which is capital and that which could be capital. In this way, capital is always a mode of *reproduction* and *exclusion*: surplus-value is produced by living labor, but the social relations that enable, insist upon, and are bolstered by the material consequences of production and circulation are never made 'for the first time.' Class indexes only *this* relation of capital and what could be, even as it's composed on the fact of what cannot be capital, that growing mass of surplus labor power that cannot be incorporated so as to make use of its potential surplus labor, and of what can no longer enter circulation, from decimated resources to overproduction's unrecuperable goods and dead factories. Such a threat is, for capital, at best a corrective. At worst, it is what it necessarily brings about yet cannot manage. However, the crucial point is that even that which can't be capital isn't so because of an essence or property of its own, because of a fundamentally 'uncapitalizable' content. It is what simply doesn't compute in this relation, the material of the contradiction thrown to the side, the slag of the dialectic, what Adorno would call the 'non-identical.' And it is the basis of the thoughts here.

As such, this title is more than a provocation, though that it is. It's intended to capture a sequence of moves. It is a description of what is the case, what has been happening for centuries: capital gives fire to the commons, lets them remain a bounded zone with the hope that it generates new sparks outside of 'market forces' and that such dynamism can be made profitable, or it burns them clear and begins laying other groundwork. It is also a gesture toward the sense of an active, changing, sparking 'commons' rather than a dwindling reserve (as in give fire to the commons, for they have long been *banal*). Lastly, it's an injunction for the real movement of communism (fire to the commons, that loathsome exception, and on to the messy, difficult fact of figuring out how to live beyond the category!). It's the last that deserves initial clarification, as I'm not questioning the force of thought or deed of groups such as the Diggers or Levellers, the necessity of struggles over access to land and water, or the ways in which histories from below have brought forth constant battles.

Rather, my drive is to trouble the concept of *the common* itself, as it is the drive of communism not to 'develop new social relations' but to dissolve this society, and its open enclosures and well-spring of phantom commonness, as such. It's on these terms that I turn to a particular corner of left communist thought, grouped around Amadeo Bordiga and those who drew from him, however 'dissidently,' including my concern here, Jacques Camatte and others associated with *Invariance*. In particular, it is Camatte's major work *Capital and Community: the results of the immediate process of production and the economic work of Marx*[146] on which I'll focus, along with a set of loose theses on form, content, and banality, on 'time's carcass' and nothing in common, and, finally, on transition at once necessary and unable to articulate where it's going.

Capital and Community begins with an extended reconstruction of aspects of Marx's project, particularly the 'autonomization of exchange value,' the relation between dead and living labor, real and formal subsumption, and a special emphasis on an interpretation of capital as 'value in process.' However, it is the set of historical and anthropological conclusions gathered in the second half that concern us, particularly the exploration of how class is no longer *coherent* the way it had been figured by major lineages of Marxism. Such is the consequence not of a perspectival shift from Marxism (as can be seen in his later work) but of an historically situated Marxist claim as to the fully transformative effects of the increasing 'autonomization' of capital. Such a claim is present in Bordiga's work as well, particularly in the discussion of the 'universal class' and the *senza riserve* (the without-reserves) that Camatte incorporates. But it's also close to a disparate set of theses, ranging from the '70's work of Italian Marxists on 'social capital' (most pointedly in Negri's 1978 lectures on the *Grundrisse*, gathered in English as *Marx Beyond Marx*) to theories of proletarianization, not just in terms of Debord's point about 'the extension of the logic of factory labor to a large sector of services and intellectual professions' but a wider-sweeping claim about the dissolution and dissemination of a previously distinct category of proletarian experience and identity.[147]

One of the major questions posed by *Capital and Community*, a question that remains arguably the dominant research of left and ultra-left communist thought, in all its different stripes, is the relation between the 'defeat of the proletariat' (i.e. the successive collapses of revolutionary movements in the 20th century) and the recomposition, or 'negation', of a previous order of class differentiation. For Camatte,

> the attempt to negate classes would have had no chance of success if there had not been another cause for its birth: the defeat of the world proletariat in the period 1926-28. Mystification means power of capital plus the defeat of the proletariat. Present-day society lives from a momentarily defeated revolution.

Excluding for the moment a longer discussion of causality and counterfactual possibility (*might that defeat have not been?*), consider this sense of a double 'defeat': first, of a concrete, however discontinuous and heterogeneous, political program of the proletariat, and second, of the particular coherency of the working class as an entity unified, or capable of coming together, by having something in common, namely, a common relationship to capital. In another sense, this might be understood as a story of decomposition, for the 'mystification' is not of the simple order of ideological inversion. Rather, it is about a dissipation of energy, a diffusion of antagonism, away from historical worker's parties into an increasingly jumbled set of alliances, temporary associations, and positions, a double consequence of that real historical defeat and a transition in the organization of capital.

However, this should be taken as a particular element, and phase, of the wider trajectory sketched by Camatte, that of the loss of the ancient (and medieval) community (*Gemeinswesen*), the subsequent slow emergence of the 'material community' of capital, and the task of the development of the 'human community' of the real domination of communism. As such, it is a story of loss and supplantation, of what has been materially, not just ideologically, displaced in the shift from communities exchanging as a whole to individuals as the arbiters – and, as laborers, the 'content' – of exchange.

The shift described is two-fold. First, from communities that exchange as communities (i.e. there is potentially exchange *between* communities) to the introduction of exchange into those communities (between individuals) and the development of a diffuse *community of exchange*. Second, the developing 'autonomization' of exchange, in the money form, begins to generate an 'outside' external to the community's relations that becomes the fully formed material community of capitalism, as value will come to subordinate property relations per se. It is the runaway outcome of the generalization of exchange: 'So exchange produces two results: the formation of money, the general equivalent that tends to autonomy; *and the autonomization of a single relation.*' In other words, the general equivalent leads to the autonomy of money as increasingly unbound from its particular applications in discrete acts of exchange, and this produces the autonomization not of money as such (the 'monetary community' as mid-stage in the domination of capital) but of the *single relation*. This relation, however, is not a relation between distinct entities: it is the single relation of singular things becoming irrelevant, as it is the general form of equivalence – *everything is in common with everything else* – that forms the real abstraction of value. This general process is what underpins Marx's notion of *money* as the real community,[148] which Camatte extends as the 'material community', the further autonomization of this double community (as general substance, i.e. medium and measure, and as external contingency) of money. This constitutes the basic position of the proletariat, which stands against capital which completes its domination by constituting itself into a material community. The proletariat's power is created by capital itself. Capital is the cause of its growth and unification, and it is also capital that creates the objective base of the new social form: communism.

For this occasion, and this occasion alone, I'm not concerned with working through the promises and consequences of his 'political' conclusion: the political act that inaugurates the 'formal domination of communism' and liberates this society toward the 'end of politics' and development of a new human community (the 'real domination of communism'), of which the party is a superstructural figuration.

Of more immediate interest is a note added in May 1972, following his theory of the formal domination of communism and, among other things, the proposition that in that period, 'No more value, man is *no longer* "time's carcass"' (emphasis mine). The note begins:

> The study of the formal domination of communism above is valid only for the period during which the communist revolution ought to take place on the basis of the formal domination of capital over society, and also, to a certain degree, for the transition period to real domination. But since the generalization of real domination world-wide (1945) this has been totally superseded.

This, then, is a calling into doubt of 'transition programs' that might imply a new bureaucratic structure and, more importantly, the scale of that anthropomorphic inversion of man and capital, the final evacuation of determinant differences that would let one speak of a human, under capital, that was 'formally' dominated but not 'really dominated' in full. In short, that retained a *content* that, however bent into and constrained by the forms of capital, was something else: a species being that was not mere instinct and biological trait, a content common and ready to be freed by the liberation of productive forces or liberation from production, to take two well-known variants.

My stress on *content* is not accidental, as a survey back through Marxist thought, and especially left-communist traditions, reveals the enormous and fraught conceptual weight invested in the opposition of *form* and *content*. It would be a mistake to pass this off as a consequence of the rhetorical utility of such terms. Running from debates about organizational form (for instance, critiques, such as Gilles Dauvé's, of councilism as preserving capitalist 'content' while swapping out the form of management) to the content of communism (and the degree to which it is positive and 'transhistorical'), to take just two indicative examples, the problem of form/content obsesses and curses communist thought. In one of its many mobilizations in Camatte's writing, we read in the 'Conclusions' of *Capital and Community*:

> However, the dialectic does not remain empty in Marxism, its presupposition is not a material, but a social, fact. It is no longer a form which can have whatever content, but that this content, being, provides it with the form. The being is the proletariat, whose emancipation is that of humanity.

This is a relatively faithful account of how form and content function in the Marxian dialectic. Following Hegel, for Marx, the active development of content gives forth to the form latent in it: form is neither an external abstraction that qualifies content nor is it a pre-existing structure of intelligibility. It emerges from the particularity of the content. Such a notion, and such a commitment to this model of form and content, is at the root of that critique of councilism mentioned, insofar as it grasps that to have 'swapped the forms' does not alter the underlying capitalist content as such, does not allow the content of communism to develop a form adequate to itself, and, lastly, mistakes capital for a problem of form, as if due to a slippage between the value *form* and 'forms of organization'.

Briefly, I want to flesh out a notorious example to give a sense of how this conceptual opposition bears on 'the common' and the degree to which we should speak of a 'content of communism,' particularly insofar as that content has to do with the flourishing of the common.[149] In *The Poverty of Philosophy*, Marx writes, 'Time is everything, man is nothing; he is, at the most, time's carcass.' This appears, initially, as just a conveniently catastrophic metaphor. However, we might read it in three ways.

1

In the loosest interpretation, that takes it primarily as a ramped up modifier of the preceding sentence concerning how 'one man during an hour is worth just as much as another man during an hour,' man is 'time's carcass' insofar as man's specificity is killed, leaving man a carcass animated by value and made to labor, simply a unit of potential activity subordinated to labor time.

2

If we recall the particularity of form and content in Marx, however, we approach a different perspective, a trajectory sketched in a single sentence. The active development, via laboring of man as labor power (the content)[150] produces the material conditions for labor time (the form). However, the perversity of capital is that this form does not remain adequate to its content. It becomes divorced from it and increasingly autonomous. But this is not the story of a form that simply takes leave from its originary content and 'becomes everything,' simply dominant. Rather, it comes to *determine* the content in a constant passage back and forth, to force it to accord with the development of that form: any opposition between form and content becomes increasingly incoherent. As such, man is time's carcass in that living labor power is *valued* only in accordance with its form: it is that form, fully developed into the general equivalence of value, alone which is of worth.

Man, the original source of that form, is a husk dominated by an abstraction with no single inventor. Form fully reenters and occupies the content as if it were dead matter, incapable of generating further adequate forms. And when it is productive to do so, time makes those bones dance.

3

Man – or rather, the *human* as more than the common man of capital – is that which is born in the death of time. It is the leftover of the collapse of capital, and it is the faint prospect, in the decomposition of the dominant social relation (the representation that mediates between labor power and labor time), of an existence that outlives capital.

We are finally in a position to return back to the question of the common.

If one recognizes, as we must, that both the 'human community' of communism and a denser form of older community life are fully displaced by the material community of capital, and, furthermore, that appeals to either seem unconvincing as scalable models of resistance capable of contesting the social relations of capital, then the only thing common to us is our incorporation into that material community. But this is not a deadening or a subtraction of what we once had: it is the construction and imposition of a common position, the production of a negative content in accordance with a universal form. Camatte writes that, 'The proletarian (what man has become) can no longer recognize himself in a human community, since it no longer exists[...] Men who have become pure spirits can rediscover themselves in the capital form without content.' Without content, indeed, insofar as content is taken to be that from which form emerges. But capital (as social relation) is nothing if not the generative collapse of a distinction between form and a content. The *common* becomes, then, the quality across individuals that is neither a form nor a content: it is the form of general equivalence taken as general content. Marx points out that 'The equivalent, by definition, is only the identity of value with itself.'[151] The full subsumption of experience to the law of equivalence, accelerated all the more during a period of the 'socialization of labor,' therefore produces with it a hollow identity that defines man, an echo chamber of value with itself. Capital founds a negative anthropology, in that the subject common to it is the subject defined only by being potentially commensurable, as source of value, with all else that exists. There is a double move described by Marx here:

> Labor capacity has appropriated for itself only the subjective conditions of necessary labor - the means of subsistence for actively producing labor capacity, i.e. for its reproduction as mere labor capacity separated from the conditions of its realization – and it has posited these conditions themselves as things, values, which confront it in an alien, commanding personification.[152]

First, 'labor capacity' (read: those who labor) only appropriates for itself 'subjective conditions': the active work of appropriation, that marks a subject, takes on only the conditions that allow it to reproduce itself as mere labor capacity. Second, even that paltry haul of subjective conditions are then posited, materially and perspectivally, as a set of hostile objects and conditions, a personification external to itself and no more. If we have something in common, it is this very motion. More bluntly, we have *nothing* in common, and not because we are atomized individuals. No, what is common across us, the reserve of common ground to which those 'without-reserves' could turn, the site on which the universal class begins,[153] is nothing but the rendering of all things as formally common to each other (belonging to none, able to be endlessly circulated and reproduced) and of ourselves as the grounding unit of that dissolution of particular content.

What, then, of those ovens? Not of the common relation between us but *the commons*, the material things around which such relations are crystallized? A first issue is raised above, in that *common* can, and often does, point not to the owned by all but rather to the potential exchange of all by all, the equivalence of what is rendered *in common* with everything else through the form of value and the medium and measure of money. Of more interest is a point initially grounded on definitions and their histories. Rather, an etymology gives a way in. Etymologies are not in themselves useful, and often denote a certain preciousness. That said, sometimes they help us say what we mean and remind us of what we have been saying in place of that.

In casual speech, *common* runs alongside *banal* as its nobler cousin. Everyday, popular, yes, but linked to a deep, rooted essence, a content that persists despite the accidents of form. *Banal* has none of that. It is gray ephemera, the stupidity of a fleeting present, what should and will be forgotten. Quotidian, forgettable, known to all but of genuine interest to none.

The word *banal* came into English from French, from the Old French *banel*, or 'communal.' But further back, in its 13th century usage, it comes from *ban*, which includes both the sense of legal control or decree and the payment for the use of a communal resource, like an oven. In other words, the oven is not common. It is banal, because it is owned by none of those who use it communally, but it is still beholden to the logic and relations of property. It is a resource for the reproduction of a form of life and masquerades as an exception to that form, if any pretence would be made about its social use.

So too so much of what we claim as 'the commons' today: they are simply banal. They are those things *still in circulation*, even as we figure them as exceptions to the regime of accumulation and enclosure. Capital has not, as some claim, rendered things common in the way that 'new social relations' could allow us to transform the logic of the present into a basis for upheaval. It has rendered all things common in that they are

187

commensurable, but the other side of the *nothing-in-common* we have become is this *pseudo-commons* of the banal. The point of communism is to develop contradictions, but this general acceleration of banality – the counterpart to the immiseration of entire populations and evisceration of resources, the tack taken by states who prefer to make social institutions 'communal' again so as to dodge the bill of social welfare spending – is neither contradiction nor generative potential. To take it as such is to simply gather around that last remaining oven, poking at its dull embers.

Despite the specificity of the volume, I have not yet spoken of *communization*, for the simple reason that I have not yet spoken of *transition*. My concern has been how we understand the position in which we find ourselves and how that relates to our discontinuous instances, what might chain them together, what forms of thought could aid that work. The notion of communization, as I understand its lineages and theoretical utility, means not that the transition to communism has already begun simply because the limits of a previous sequence of working-class struggles are becoming unavoidable. Nor does it mean that it *can* begin at our behest, through the development of practices of being in common and making common, through the commune as form and through doubled tactics of expropriation and sharing, resulting in a local withdrawal of singularities (bodies and commodities as stripped of exchange value) from circulation. Rather, it is a theory that casts doubt on the notion of *transition* and that concerns what used to be called a revolutionary period. I am not alone in severely doubting the degree to which, given the current geopolitical order, any notion of a 'general revolution against capital' obtains. Uprisings, revolts, and insurrections seem even less likely now than previously to be 'about' value in any explicit way: if anything, a more precise theory should make sense of how the apparent, and real, *content* of historically determined struggles over democratic representation, outright repression of the populace, racism and patriarchy, food shortages, changes in pension and retirement law, denial of social services, real wages, and ecological catastrophe have already and will continue to run into an increasing set of deadlocks shaped by the limits of the material and social *form* of the reproduction of capital. Despite this, one of the values of guarding a notion of 'revolution' is that it marks a distinct sequence that exacerbates and explodes a set of given conditions and that cannot be produced ex nihilo by radical practices.

If the contradictions of capital generate a cursed dialectic of form and content, such that the form dominates the content at the same time that it cannot be separated from it, the elaboration of communist thought and strategy is to inflect and impel this worsening contradiction. Not to pathetically cheer at the failure of 'reformist' struggles and not to scour them in the hopes of finding the common element hidden in them, but to see in them the determined contours of the relations of capital, the demands placed on those bodies that work and die, the representations that bind together and mediate 'the material conditions to blow this foundation sky-high.' The vicious fact of it is that it simply is not our decision. We choose a period of capital as much as we choose an earthquake. Yet to make of this a *principle*, not of withdrawal but of holding on and forth: such would be a courage and a line worth taking. To hate the ruined and the unruined alike, with neither fetish nor indifference, to know that we cannot make our time, but that it does not, and never will, unfold untouched. Communization, then, is not an option we choose to take, but it is not an inevitability. It is a situation that will present itself, given the limits of capital, and it is a situation that has no guarantee of 'leading to communism.' To say that such a state of affairs will come to pass is very different from saying *how* they will come to pass, how the necessary measures taken by what has no reserve will happen, and what kind of resistance, physical and intellectual, they meet and for how long.

The concept of invariance is an important one for the Bordigist tradition on which I've drawn, and it remains one today, though not in the sense of a transhistorical organizational form, a universal communist content, or unchanging line of attack and analysis. Rather, I mean the invariance of this sort of principle, persisting across transformations, that refuses to look 'elsewhere,' to a far past or future after capital, to ground any communist project and that insists that *things will not unfold as we expect them to.* Between those material reversals and inversions of communization, we can expect only that there will be difficult losses and gains. Not the quick falling away of forms of thought or the development of new relations as such, but a falling apart of what we've come to expect 'resistance' to look like and the coming forth of what had no place before. And moreover, a recognition that the processes of the decay and dismantling of social relations, and the world built in their image, can only be messy, contradictory, and frequently incoherent.

All the more reason for us to be rigorous, to keep clear heads, to build up the kind of analyses and practices that may be of use or necessity. Because one cannot exclude from those infamous 'objective conditions' all that constitutes the given terrain of a period, including an enormous set of 'subjective' and 'affective' conditions: words that have been in the air, that sense of things getting worse at work, home, and in the streets, successes and failures of struggles over wages, reproductive rights, and access to social services, the networks and connections built between comrades over years, attacks on minorities and immigrants, the skills and resources we have or take, the social habits of the rich, the trends of cultural production, and a learned familiarity of not knowing if a day will start and end in a world that feels remotely the same. It is the deadlocks, impasses, and cracks composed of *all* of this that are our concern. For such a time of catastrophe breaks onto a shore that's never a bare fact of economy. We're ground down and smoothed, sure, such that we become channels or levies designed to simply mitigate, but our thinking and fighting inflect that break all the same. In this way, the intellectual and material practice of what could be called the Party is, at its best, a general *angle of inflection.* It is an exertion of pressure that makes us capable of reading in the scattered field of breakdowns a correlation, a fraying pattern from which our modes cannot be separated.

For communism has no content, and it is not form. It is *decomposi-*

tion. It is the mass, committed, and uncertain undoing of the representations that mediate form and content, time and labor, value and property, and all the real relations that sustain between them. It begins not outside, before, or after, but right there, with the absent content of having nothing in common. It starts in times when a set of material limits show themselves as being unsurpassable other than by a practical appropriation of necessary goods and an accompanying rejection of social forms. Such times do and will come, though not everywhere at once. How it will go is hard to say. But we should not forget that when bodies decompose and start to fall apart, they give off heat, loosing that energy bound up and frozen in its particular arrangement. That carcass of time, the subject of equivalence, is one such shape, petrified as it may appear. At the least, let's stop coming back to the scorched village and the banal oven, stop blowing on its cold coals. Let's gather around that corpse instead and warm our hands there, over the hot wind rising from the end of the common and the start of a slow thaw a long time coming.

9

Make Total Destroy
John Cunningham

> Everything cleared away means to the destroyer a complete reduction, indeed eradication, of his own condition.
> Walter Benjamin, *The Destructive Character.*[154]

I've always liked the phrase 'make total destroy' both for its apt summation of the affective resonance of being submerged in capitalism and its a-grammatical punk elegance. The phrase is apparently 'an old Anarchist in-joke referencing the mangled English and almost self-parodying militant image of the Greek Anarchists.'[155] For all that, destructive negation has never been so well expressed. However, the State's capacity to manage and control the most necessary acts of resistance in terms of blockades, riots, demonstrations and occupations shouldn't be underestimated. Contemporary capitalism's state of exception has yet to be punctured or disabled by a praxis of unalloyed negation, however militant. Ignoring this can lead to an aestheticization of destruction – black bloc images, textual declarations of social war – at odds with any capacity to institute such measures.

But where does this leave communization? As the eradication of the very ground upon which the structural violence of capital is erected communization is seemingly the most relentlessly destructive of contemporary anticapitalist tendencies. The anti-productivist seizure of the productive apparatus and the destruction of any notion of the 'proletariat' and 'commodity' would lead to an absolute rupture and break with capitalism. As Gilles Dauvé writes, communization 'does not take the old material bases as it finds them: it overthrows them.'[156] Communization is the negation of all the elements of capital without a transitional 'workers' state', and a revolutionary process which is itself communism. The breaking of the reproductive cycle of our needs being based on maintaining capitalism would itself be an integrated process of the communizing of production and social reproduction. Communization would be an almost unimaginable throwing into question of what production and social reproduction might mean. As such, the destructive moment of communization would be qualitatively different from what's thought of as political violence. Tracing this line of negation in communization might illuminate both communization and concepts of destructive negation in earlier anticapitalist theorizations of political violence, as well as figuring out in what other ways 'make total destroy' might be understood.

An Anti-Political Violence?

One question that needs to be immediately addressed is the role a simplistic valorization of 'make total destroy' plays in simply reproducing the capitalist social relation in anticapitalist milieus. In the 1970s French ultra-leftist Jacques Camatte linked the uncritical valorization of a negation predicated upon violence with 'repressive consciousness' – the elevation of theory and a 'militant' subjectivity into a self-identification with revolutionary praxis.[157] This can actually block the emergence of revolt and submerge it within what Camatte termed 'rackets' of anticapitalist enterprise. All too often an identification of anti-capitalism with destructive negation fulfils this role. The actual end of an identification with violent negation would be the perpetuation of a particular form of 'revolutionary' organization – the degeneration into clandestine resistance or an ideological sect being the apex of this – or simply the affirmation of extremity as a stylistic gesture. That a communizing anti-politics would reject the institutional left – in favour of more diffuse forms of resistance such as wildcat strikes, blockades and occupations – could almost be taken for granted but this anti-politics should also be present in a critique that deactivates any nascent 'repressive consciousness'. The anti-political violence implicit within communization – even on a theoretical level – should be corrosive of 'repressive consciousness' and 'rackets'. Both help reproduce the conditions of capitalism and its constituent systemic violence in the form of a self-perpetuating conflict managed by 'rackets'.

Camatte's caveat about violence is that 'each individual must be violent with him/ herself in order to reject [...] the domestication of capital and all its comfortable, self-validating "explanations"'.[158] I think this suggests that the rejection of the 'domestication of capital' by the 'individual' would be based upon studying the effects of the material processes of capital upon the 'subjective'. Critique itself would be filtered through the prism of abstraction. A complimentary approach is suggested by Walter Benjamin in the essay 'Critique of Violence', where he writes that: 'The critique of violence is the philosophy of its history [...] Because only the idea of its development makes possible a critical, discriminating, and decisive approach to this temporal data.'[159] Any theorisation of destructive negation should conceptualise it formally through the abstractions of 'the philosophy of its history'. The existence of violence in capitalism provides the condition for a critique that acts through abstraction in order to avoid 'repressive consciousness'. Such an exercise isn't just genealogical – the tracing of a conceptual history – but is also an attempt to ensure that a false immediacy in valorizing destructive negation is deactivated and doesn't reproduce 'repressive consciousness'. The 'philosophy' of the brief history of communization as a theoretical praxis is best tracked through looking at the questions raised around 'programmatism' by Théorie Communiste (TC).

Periodizing Destruction

What could be called the communization tendency in anticapitalism is in no way homogenous, and extends from the ultra-left influenced Troploin (Gilles Dauvé and Karl Nesic), Endnotes, TC and Bruno Astarian, through to the post-Tiqqun milieu. The latter strand complicates the image of any communizing theoretical praxis by both productively incorporating the bio-political insights of Agamben and Foucault alongside a problematically naïve impetus towards a secessionist exit from existent social relations.[160] Both share a similar impetus towards and emphasis upon the negative, with the former tracking communization through the varied structural contradictions of contemporary capitalism and the latter emphasising an active – if poetic – nihilism. It's the former, more Marxist theoretical praxis within communization – especially TC – that seem to draw out the particular nature of negation as destruction within communization. This is evident when the question of periodization is considered, though there's a wide divergence especially between Troploin and TC over the historical specificity of communization.[161] As opposed to Troploin's relatively invariant Marxist humanism TC emphasise that communization is a break with the past. This is conceptualised by TC in terms of the decomposition of 'programmatism'.

In brief, 'programmatism' is the forms of organization (mass parties, unions) and ideologies (socialism and syndicalism) that valorized workers' power – often expressed in a program of measures to be implemented after the revolution – and were emblematic of the 19th and 20th century workers' movement. TC argue that with an intensification of 'real subsumption' – essentially the submergence of the entirety of society within a self-positing capitalism – in the 1970s the 'old' workers' movement and proletariat become further imbricated within the reproduction of capitalism. Rather than the proletariat constituting an 'outside' to capital and feasting off its corpse, both decompose together in a shifting matrix of mutual need and opposition within the twin cycles of the reproductive shredding mechanism that TC term the 'double moulinet'.[162] This has the added appetiser that the workers' movement carried within itself its antagonist in the shape of a reconstitution of capitalism in the very form its resistance takes – the valorization of the proletariat. Such a symmetrical opposition between a positively defined proletariat and the capitalist class risks simply replacing the management of capitalism through the exercise of force. And such a scenario would just replicate a *political* violence that remains locked into perpetuating particular apparatuses of power and force even if in the shape of supposedly anticapitalist milieus, parties, organizations, etc.

TC have traced the imbrication of capital within the particular forms that resistance might take in the present as communization. Whatever the problems of being overly schematic in periodization – such as the temptation of determinism – the thesis of 'programmatism' is useful in delineating what a communizing 'make total destroy' might be. The destructive negation of communization is partly embodied in the violence of this break with the past of the 'old' workers' movement – particularly so with TC. This inheres in a rejection of both past forms of organization as having any revolutionary agency and in a lack of any nostalgia for any of the supposed verities of 'workers' power'. Instead, communization posits a proletariat that negates itself as an element of capitalism through a crisis of the reproductive cycle that entwines capital and proletariat together. To untie the reproductive knot that strangles the proletariat is not a matter of freeing a productive proletarian essence that's being constrained. It's more a case of strangling both proletariat and capital as reciprocal elements of the constraints of this reproductive cycle.

Of course, the thesis of 'programmatism' is nuanced by also

being an attempt to understand the present through the past in order to understand what – if anything – is possible in the present. Communization in this sense remains a speculative wager as to a slow and uneven process of proletarian dis-identification and revolt being produced through capital's own often abortive attempts at self-valorization. Communization isn't predicated upon the affirmation of any existent aspect of capitalism such as the proletariat or, for that matter, nebulous entities such as the 'multitude'. It represents a break with both the remnants of the 'old' workers movement and other strands of 'anticapitalism' in the present almost as much as it posits a break with capital. But negation as destruction can itself be periodized and contextualised. The decomposition of 'programmatism' and the accompanying shift from a proletariat that sought to valorize itself to confronting itself as a limit is also a shift in how to conceptualize destruction. With this negation as destruction is an involution of itself as any opposition to capital ultimately necessitates a dissolution of being proletariat. Likewise, the question of representation and the state is dissolved through this since there's nothing to 'represent' within a process of communization.

This periodization of destructive negation can be compared with another, antagonistic, figure – the philosopher Alain Badiou. In his work he traces the link between destruction and negation, regarding negation as a subordinate process in the affirmation and creation of the new.[163] Badiou serves as a place marker for the cycles of anticapitalist resistance that the theorization of communization also emerged from. In a particularly singular register his experience and responses encapsulate both the post-'68 milieu that entered into conflict with the 'old' workers' movement, as well as attempts to formalise post-Seattle anticapitalism. He had his own moment of valorizing destruction as a post-'68 Maoist in his work *Theory of the Subject* (1982): 'Destroy [...] such is the necessary – and prolonged – proletarian statement'.[164] There's a suggestive hint in *Theory of the Subject* that through its emphasis upon the destruction of 'splace' – the place that produces proletarian subjectivity – that Badiou shares something with early formulations of communization. However, as with much post-'68 leftism there's a tension in *Theory of the Subject* that strains against the limits of 'programmatism' but still collapses back into some form of the party. Badiou's Maoism – an ideology that seems almost parodic in the present – led him at the time to tying revolutionary subjectivity into the radical subject of the 'proletarian' party rather than a more diffuse proletarian resistance.

Tracing Badiou's shifting response to the aporia of the decomposition of 'programmatism' we find a shift from a politics of destruction, outlined in the 1970s and early 1980s, to a new theorization of 'subtractive' communism from the later 1980s to the present. Destruction is posited as an 'indefinite task of purification' towards a 'real' obscured by ideology, capitalism, etc., and is associated by Badiou with the politics of the 'passion for the real' of the left revolutionary and artistic movements of the 20th century.[165] It is the exhaustion of this sequence, for Badiou, that leads him towards 'subtraction' as the attempt to avoid the 'disaster' of an over-identification with the necessarily violent aspect of negation, and instead to emphasize negation as a creative process. 'Subtraction' carefully inscribes limits into what is achievable. Reformatting the shape of radical politics in an unpropitious context, Badiou centers it on 'subtraction' as a communism of withdrawal into the construction of a 'minimal difference' – an emancipatory politics 'subtracted' from economics and the state. Practically, this means yet more supposedly 'autonomous' spaces and militant but post-Bolshevik forms of organization. But this 'subtractive' anticapitalism also constitutes one of the limits of the present that communization is attempting a highly-contingent exit from. While subtraction as a communism of withdrawal tries to avoid the 'repressive consciousness' of a reified negation, it replaces this with its own alternative militant forms that elide the problem of negation.

The theoretical praxis of communization upsets Badiou's schema of a passage from destruction to subtraction, and it would be a mistake to identify communization with an outdated politics of destruction. Communization's positing of the eradication of the very predicates of capitalism is embedded within the recognition that a 'subtractive' communism of the kind Badiou touts is an impossibility when all social relations are mediated through capital. From the perspective of communization Badiou's formal distinction collapses as destruction and subtraction are in fact so closely intertwined as to be indistinguishable – new forms of social relations being produced directly through the anti-productivist destruction of capitalism. One of the conditions for the exit from the present posited through communization is recognition of our embedding in the wider economy of violence that constitutes capitalism. This is a *Gewalt* that communization as destructive negation needs to be situated within.

Real Abstract Violence

Capitalism has its own forms of structural violence, succinctly defined by Étienne Balibar as the 'violence of economics and the economics of violence.'[166] Such a violence is the *Gewalt* of capital. *Gewalt* is an ambiguous, multifaceted term that describes the immanence of force, violence and power within the social field of capitalism. *Gewalt* encompasses both the legitimised force and violence of the state, always at hand to coercively ensure exploitation continues, and the violence implicit in the process of proletarianization that's the result of labor being abstracted from bodies and intellect as labor power. A slogan that thought and acted with the event of the Greek uprising in 2008 is succinct about this: 'VIOLENCE means working for 40 years, getting miserable wages and wondering if you ever get retired...'[167] It's this definition of 'violence', along with precarity, disciplinary welfare systems, needing-hating wage labor, etc. that make me think 'make total destroy' needs to be considered as a component of communization. This violence of state and capital are analogous but not identical. They come together in both the coercion – subtle or otherwise – necessary for the reproduction of capitalism as a social relation and in periods of primitive accumulation. Balibar's erudite genealogical study of *Gewalt* in Marx and anticapitalism revolves around the ambiguities implicit in any use of *Gewalt*. Even in oppositional anticapitalist forms it could just be the reproduction of a symmetrical relation of force and violence that remains within capitalism. This is embodied in the instrumentality of such violence whether capitalist or anticapitalist, *Gewalt* as the telos of history or just reciprocal force.

Balibar ends with a question of how to 'civilize' the revolution and step out of a systemic use of force and violence. There's no need to follow Balibar into his reappraisal of Gandhi and some notion of 'civilization' – whatever that might mean – to recognize the pertinence of discovering an oppositional *Gewalt* that doesn't reproduce the structural constraints of the force and violence of capitalism. Whether revolt should be 'civilizing' or a new kind of barbarism seems beside the point. Civilization and associated terms such as progress and humanism have long carried the baggage for nothing much more than the extraction of value from laboring bodies. An oppositional *Gewalt* would be one that irrevocably broke this systemic violence and there's no need to enter into the ethical labyrinth of how 'civilizing' this needs to be in order to break with such an emptied out 'progress'. The question of choosing between 'civilization' and 'barbarism' isn't one that's really posed to those caught within the *Gewalt* of capitalism. The *Gewalt* within capitalism maintains itself as a ghostly systemic presence even if often unacknowledged or elided by many states in favour of a language of formal 'human rights'. More than this, 'human rights' remain inscribed within the logic of *Gewalt* and are constitutive of it; as Benjamin notes defeated subjects are 'accorded rights even when the victors superiority in power is complete'.[168] *Gewalt* is in no way a fault or objective failure within capitalism as might be supposed by liberals but an exception that's always already included within it as essential to its functioning.

Violence within capitalism isn't just the coercive police violence of the state but also acts through the abstractions – such as money and value

– that constitute it as a social relation. Such real abstractions dissolve the boundaries between concrete and abstract, the 'real' and ideology, subjective and objective.[169] Luca Basso writes that Marx's conceptualization of *Gewalt* encapsulates 'the idea of a violent subjection, not only in the sense of brutal force, but also in that apparently more tenuous one of abstract and impersonal rule.'[170] The cop that beats demonstrators, the monthly wage – or lack of it – and the overall mediation of human relations through value are all aspects of *Gewalt*. While violence has its own abstraction within capitalism its actual effects are anything but. In a sense the state and less 'abstract' aspects of domination are mediated through the value-form as the state plays its role within this. *Gewalt* intertwines both capital and the state in an endlessly repeated accumulation of resources and the re-production of the existent social relation. As such this is always a means to this specific end, but it's not quite as simple as a pure instrumentality of violence. In terms of the totality of capitalism this 'end' is also in itself a process towards the realization of surplus-value for capital. As Postone writes 'the expenditure of labor power is not a means to another end, but, as a means has become an end'.[171] The 'end' is the undead becoming of capital itself, an ever self-perpetuating inhuman subject that overdetermines all other forms of life.

But what happens when this reproductive cycle begins to break down? Capitalism has its own 'make total destroy' in the shape of the de-valorization, the supposedly 'creative destruction' of fixed capital – technology, factories and infrastructure – and labor power, or more simply people. Capital creates its own wastelands in order to perpetuate itself and attempts to manage its own crises through generalizing them into a general crisis of social reproduction. TC write in the *Glass Floor*, a recent text on the Greek uprising: 'Absurdly, the wage and the reproduction of labor-power tend to become illegitimate for capital itself... This is the crisis of reproduction, the running out of future.'[172]

We have the double spectre of runaway capitalism. One is the spiral of capital becoming fictitious, positing itself upon its own over accumulation in packages of debt and attempting to unchain itself from labor-power as a basis for the accumulation of surplus value. The other reciprocal spectre is that of a unilateral uncoupling by capital of our ability to 'enjoy' the suffering of the violence of the wage relation, and so our ability to even reproduce ourselves as its subjects. Michael Denning has suggested that the paradigm to understand capital is that of a 'wageless life' predicated upon the reproduction of informal and precarious forms of labor whether in shanty towns or the advanced sectors of the capitalist economy.[173] Whereas Denning argues that this was possibly always the case, and so risks freezing 'wageless life' into an eternally fixed condition, it does capture what's at stake in this reproductive crisis. His linking of 'wageless life' to Marx's characterisation of the free laborer as a 'virtual pauper' always potentially surplus to capitals requirements expresses not so much the objective decadence of capitalism but rather its continual restructuring.[174] The destructive negation of communization is an attempt to grasp the possibilities within this moment.

The classic response of the Left would be an attempt to reinstitute wage labor as a precondition for social reproduction, but communization as a theoretical praxis is intertwined with and inhabits the contemporary nexus of devalorization, the decomposition of class, and the mutually the imbricated reproductive cycles of capital and labor. Rather than somehow stepping out of the immanent *Gewalt* of capitalism – an impossibility – communization might be seen as an oppositional praxis that turns this *Gewalt* against itself. It's very much in this sense that communization contains the necessity of destruction and traces its possibilities through it – not as the acceleration of capital's catastrophism, but as the positing of a different means without end to capital's attempt to posit itself as an endlessly reproducing self-valorizing process.

Pure Means

The problematic of means and ends preoccupied Walter Benjamin in his essay 'Critique of Violence' in what initially seems a different register from that of capitals self-positing *Gewalt*. He made a distinction between a 'mythic' violence subordinated to the 'legal' ends of the state and a 'divine' or 'sovereign' violence that was decoupled from the question of ends. Benjamin's deconstruction of the aporia of a state based *Gewalt* and his ascent – or descent – into a theology of 'sovereign violence' seems like an unpromising place to formulate the very different problematic of communization. In some ways Benjamin inevitably remains very much of his time. The concept of a 'sovereign violence' is theorized through the distinction made by the syndicalist Sorel between the 'political' strike and the 'proletarian general strike'. The former is a legitimised violence over pay and conditions, and even at its most radical it only results in a new 'law' or state overseen by the representatives of the workers. Conversely the 'proletarian general strike' would show an 'indifference to a material gain through conquest' and result in what Benjamin termed a 'wholly transformed work, no longer enforced by the state'.[175] In a sense this is the limit of Benjamin's then contemporary example of the syndicalist 'proletarian general strike', in that as it approaches production there's still a drift towards the affirmation of work and proletarian identity, even while breaking out of the cycle of a violence that would always re-institute the state.

Even so, within this formulation there's a trace of what a communizing *Gewalt* might be. In conceptualizing the 'proletarian general strike' Benjamin pushed against these limits and arrived at a point of mapping a violence that would be a 'pure means'. A 'pure means' would only find its justification within its own activity and would change social relations without being affixed to an 'end' or any particular teleology. So, against the quantitative 'end' of the realization of surplus value as a process in itself such a 'pure means' posits the possibility of a self-perpetuating *Gewalt* that breaks with the exigencies of value production. It is in this sense that 'pure means' suggests an oppositional *Gewalt* as a decomposition of the binary structure of the violence that would lead to the reinstitution of a new state that it relates to communization. The redefinition of the very notion of violence as it secedes from the *Gewalt* of capitalism means that it is no longer 'violence' but a cessation of the dynamics of violence through the 'proletarian general strike' – a blockade and sabotage of the economic violence of capitalism that circulates materials, bodies and commodities in order to produce value. It's tempting to see a trace of this in the most petty – and often involuntary – blockages of the reproduction of capitalism, whether through workplace theft or simply not working when at work. What Benjamin described as the weakened 'pure means' of the political strike is in fact a product of an attempt to forestall wider practices of sabotage, as he writes: 'Did not workers previously resort at once to sabotage and set fire to factories?'[176] But more significantly, the reproductive crisis of the 'double moulinet' contains within it an involuntary break such as this when through crises the interlocking cyclical shredding of human material pulls apart.

However, 'pure means' is an ambiguous concept in Benjamin's thought. In another register he links 'pure means' to a mob violence that institutes its own justice outside of the norms of law, and so 'sovereign violence' retains the sense of an unmediated violence. This discomforting association suggests to me a limitation in Benjamin's thought, as the violent rupture of 'pure means' becomes a vitalist anarchism, a purely subjective and voluntarist break with capitalism. While this at least breaks apart any neat conceptual sophistries that deny the violence internal to 'pure means', it leaves it reduced to remaining trapped as nothing but the expression of tensions within a capitalist *Gewalt*, and not an oppositional break with it. Also, given that all violence is mediated through the *Gewalt* of capital the suggestion of such an unmediated violence loses something of the kind of rupture suggested by the 'proletarian general strike.' Not that this is necessarily non-violent in its totality, but such a violence is simultaneously mediated through capital as a negation while breaking with it – such a 'pure means' or 'sovereign violence' would be expressed in its social form as both a continuous process and in its actual expression as *Gewalt*. TC note that in such an interconnected process, wherein value is abolished, 'one can't distinguish between the activity of strikers and insurgents, and the creation of other relations between individuals'.[177] This violence would be embedded in more than the activity of a radical minority and be a rupture with the social relations that constitute the *Gewalt* of capital.

'Pure means' would then be expressed through a decoupling of proletarian social reproduction from the reproduction of capital through a very material process that would dismantle both the capitalist productive apparatus and the subjective limits that it imposes upon forms of life. However, production as production – machinery, technology and bodies producing value through work – remains under-theorized within the philosophical discourse of 'pure means'. Giorgio Agamben – who has extrapolated from Benjamin's initial formulation – only discusses production and 'pure means' when he relates production to the act of shitting. He writes humorously that 'feces are a human production like any other',[178] before more seriously arguing for a collective 'profanation' of the products of capitalism since an individual one would be 'parodic'. It's worth staying with Agamben's parodic image of shit as emblematic of capitalist production in order to elaborate upon production and 'pure means'. At the beginning of Elio Petri's 1971 film *The Working Class Goes to Heaven* the main protagonist – a heroically hard-working factory worker – discusses production in the same terms as Agamben but more astutely. Comparing his body to the factory he imagines the production of feces as being akin to the production of commodities and his own mind as being capital. The production process of the factory and his own bodily identity as proletarian constitute the same limit and have the same result – shit. In one sense a purely negative anthropology underpins communization. Proletarianization is experienced as a constitutive lack, a hollowing out predicated upon exploitation rather than any positive political identity.

Communization is the anti-product of this constitutive lack, but this hollowed out substratum reduced to abstract labor exists in a tension with a *potenzia* that isn't some vitalist essence but a negative potentiality more revealed through the destructive negation of these limits as a communizing pure means. The anti-productivist imperative of communization constitutes a 'make total destroy', which is projected as the resolution and negation of the *Gewalt* of capitalism. In the present this is much more easily apprehended in the negative, as we remain inevitably trapped within a *Gewalt* defined through capitalism. In the shape of anti-productivism the theoretical praxis of communization directly approaches the conjunction of 'pure means' and a destructive negation that mirrors the devalorization of capital, except it's in the form of a devalorization that breaks the existent social relation. The speculative theorization of this as 'gratuity' suggests it carries a hidden cargo that's the dissolution of the subjective limits of the existent social relation through the collapse of the 'double moulinet'.

The notion of gratuity in the work of TC and Bruno Astarian brings together 'pure means' and communization in a way that can be grasped in the present. This is the more speculative side of communization, in that the negative import of the present is unfolded into a transformation of social relations. Gratuity is the forcible appropriation of commodities on the basis of need and their subsequent destruction as commodities. Gratuity could be a 'pure means' in insurrectionary activity in the present – as with proletarian shopping – but the notion could also be intensified as a broader and more intense negation:

> The attack against the capitalist nature of the means of production is tantamount to their abolition as value absorbing labor in order to valorize itself; it is the extension of gratuity, the potentially physical destruction of certain means of production; their abolition as factories in which the product is defined as product.[179]

The theoretical praxis of communization postulates an active destruction through the seizure of factories, technologies, and commodities as part of a transformation of social relations. Those shiny assemblages of enticing commodities and the harsher realities of assembly line production that dominate our world would not just be appropriated or placed under a new 'anticapitalist' management. The very notion of 'product' and 'production' would be trashed in this process and replaced by the realization of social relations no longer trapped under the object of realizing value, or any object whatsoever.

'Gratuity' is a communizing *Gewalt* that breaks with the coercive structural violence of capitalism that's reiterated through the imposition of a crisis in social reproduction. It dissolves the boundaries between production and social reproduction in a re-inscription of 'pure means' as a negation of the mediation of the value-form. Bruno Astarian writes in a much more speculative register that: 'Gratuity is gratuity of the activity (in the sense that its productive result is secondary). It is freedom of access to one's living conditions (including the means of "production" and "consumption").'[180] In gratuity there's an expenditure of force unrelated to the 'economic' as factories, offices, universities, etc. are torn away from their place as sites for the reproduction of capitalism. This is a negation that decomposes the apparatuses that comprise a capitalist *Gewalt*, as well as opening up, destroying and distributing what was previously constrained within exchange-value. Simultaneously, Astarian argues that such insurrectionary activity is productive of new forms of subjectivity predicated upon a disaffiliation with being proletarian. The closed loop of the capitalized subject opens out into a collective and individual resistance that's intent upon discovering new ways of satisfying the means of social reproduction. This would be an asymmetrical move out of an anticapitalist resistance that remains caught within defending such sites in the present out of our necessity to exist within capitalism.

Gratuity would be the strongest expression of 'pure means' as an activity that was founded upon itself and expresses nothing but this. Bruno

Astarian extends this to the notion of a 'production without production', wherein material production is secondary to the transformation of social relations. Perhaps the utopian Fourier is the hidden referent and underpinning of all this negation and destruction – as Pierre Klossowski wrote 'Fourier envisaged an economy of abundance resulting [...] in the free play of passions'.[181] A productive relation based around affect and the passions sounds impossibly utopian but given that contemporary spectacular capitalism is partially driven by instrumentalizing affect and 'the passions' it might not be so utopian to imagine the opposite.

The anti-productivism of gratuity could be taken as communization being a utopia of machine-breakers and bring it uncomfortably close to some form of primitivism. Compared to the emphasis upon the 'progressive' role of the forces of production and their restraint by the relations of production in more traditional Marxism communization does present a break. This could be linked to simply fetishizing the destruction of technology, but within the theoretical praxis of communization is less to do with this than with the way productive forces as determined by capital feed back into the exploitation. As Dauvé notes communization dissolves the 'dictatorship of production relations over society',[182] and 'Make total destroy' would be the inversion of the productive apparatus into a means of producing new social relations, or perhaps more accurately a destruction that negates the constraining mesh of exchange value and subjects existing forms to a communizing relation without measure.

The Limits of Pure Means

Conceptualizing communization in terms of 'pure means' also demonstrates its limits in the present. An anti-productivist destruction as 'pure means' can only be apprehended as a negative image of the present – the potential breaking of the limits of existent capitalism. Acknowledging this is a good way of avoiding Benjamin's occasional mysticism about 'sovereign violence' as not being recognisable in the profane world. The projected anti-productivist destruction that communization would take is mediated negatively through capital, but a 'pure means' in the present is only ever a trace of this. For instance, Giorgio Agamben's elaboration of 'pure means' is that it's the 'creation of a new use [made] possible only by deactivating an old use, rendering it inoperative'.[183] Negation is inscribed within 'pure means', though it's a weakened, playful negation that reveals itself through any act that is a détournement of the apparatuses of social control. Just as the *Gewalt* inscribed within capitalism isn't the pure application of brute force so a communizing *Gewalt* can't be reduced to a violent insurrection. For instance, a *Gewalt* as 'pure means' might be embodied in the present within a praxis that refuses to demand anything and refuses to enter into the paradigm of 'human rights'. A limit to this is that 'no demands' can become a demand in itself and reinstitute a 'repressive consciousness' amongst a radical minority. 'No demands' can only be a trace of the generalised 'no demand' that would be communization.

It's also tempting to relate 'pure means' to phenomena such as the practice of 'proletarian shopping' that was common in Italy in the 1970s. The self-reduction of prices, or en masse looting of shops, is a 'pure means' in that it produces new ways for people to relate to one another outside of exchange as well as being an improvised response to the pressures of social reproduction by playfully voiding the act of consumerism. Such an activity is what Agamben terms a 'profanation' of the gilded, 'sacred' commodities that define contemporary consumer capitalism. Agamben's emphasis upon détournement suggests the way that even the concept of violence might shift in a praxis of 'pure means'. This improvisational quality may even be its main advantage over the more symmetrical forms of a classic application of *Gewalt*. But détournement might also be the limit of Agamben's notion of 'pure means.' Even if such activity is engaged in the crises around social reproduction it remains trapped within the already established circulation of commodities, money and other shit within capitalism.[184] It doesn't penetrate the 'glass floor' of production identified by TC as a limit to contemporary resistance.[185]

This is further complicated by a double bind of biopolitics wherein the lack of a subject defined through exploitation is mirrored by an almost parodic subjective plenitude, as identities based around consumption, work, ethnicity, sexuality, etc., are reproduced through apparatuses composed of discourses, institutions and technologies. Apparatuses reproduce a more uneven terrain of struggle that includes but can't be reduced to production as a site of contestation, corresponding to the everyday and potentially blocking insurrection. This aporia will only be resolved through a praxis that disables the entire reproductive cycle of capital and what that would be remains an open question. 'Make Total Destroy' emerges through the theoretical praxis of communization as always already filtered through the *Gewalt* of contemporary capitalism and it's this that makes it a highly contingent negation. An anti-productivist, anti-political 'pure means' that could decompose and decelerate the antimonies of capitalist *Gewalt* awaits its realisation through the conditions that give rise to it.

No Future?

10

Communization and the Abolition of Gender
Maya Andrea Gonzalez[186]

> Present day civilization makes it plain that it will only permit
> sexual relationships on the basis of a solitary, indissoluble bond
> between one man and one woman, and that it does not like sexual-
> ity as a source of pleasure in its own right and is only prepared to
> tolerate it because there is so far no substitute for it as a means of
> propagating the human race.
> Sigmund Freud, *Civilization and Its Discontents*

Communization is not a revolutionary position. It is not a form of society
we build after the revolution. It is not a tactic, a strategic perspective, an
organization, or a plan. Communization describes a set of measures that
we must take in the course of the class struggle *if there is to be a revolution at all*. Communization abolishes the capitalist mode of production,
including wage-labor, exchange, the value form, the state, the division of
labor and private property. That the revolution must take this form is a
necessary feature of class struggle today. Our cycle of struggles can have no
other horizon, since the unfolding contradictions of capitalism annihilated
the conditions which other forms of revolution required. It is no longer
possible to imagine a situation in which social divisions are dissolved *after*
the revolution.

Since the revolution as communization must abolish all divisions within social life, it must also abolish gender relations – not because gender is inconvenient or objectionable, but because it is part of the totality of relations that daily reproduce the capitalist mode of production. Gender, too, is constitutive of capital's central contradiction, and so gender must be torn asunder in the process of the revolution. We cannot wait until after the revolution for the gender question to be solved. Its relevance to our existence will not be transformed slowly – whether through planned obsolescence or playful deconstruction, whether as the equality of gender identities or their proliferation into a multitude of differences. On the contrary, in order to be revolution at all, communization must destroy gender *in its very course*, inaugurating relations between individuals defined in their singularity.

The fact that revolution takes the form of communization is not the result of lessons learned from past defeats, nor even from the miserable failure of past movements to solve the gender question. Whether or not we can discern, after the fact, a winning strategy for the movements of the past says nothing about the present. For capital no longer organizes a unity among proletarians on the basis of their common condition as wage-laborers. The capital-labor relation no longer allows workers to affirm their *identity* as workers and to build on that basis workers' organizations capable of assuming power within the state. Movements that elevated workers to the status of a revolutionary subject were still 'communist', but communist in a mode that cannot be ours today. The revolution as communization has no revolutionary subject, no affirmable identity – not the Worker, the Multitude, or the Precariat. The real basis of any such revolutionary identity has melted away.

Of course, workers still exist as a class. Wage-labor has become a universal condition of life as never before. However, the proletariat is diffuse and fractured. Its relation to capital is precarious. The structural oversupply of labor is enormous. A surplus population of over one-billion people – eager to find a place in the global commodity chains from which they have been excluded – makes it impossible to form mass organizations capable of controlling the supply of labor, except among the most privileged strata of workers.[187] Capital now exacerbates, fragments and more than ever relies on the divisions between workers. Once the proud bearers of a universally relevant revolutionary essence, the Working Class, in its autonomy as a class within capitalism, can no longer build its power as a class against capital. Today, *the revolution must emerge from the disunity of the proletariat, as the only process capable of overcoming that disunity.* If revolutionary action does not immediately abolish all divisions between proletarians, then it is not revolutionary; it is not communization.

In the present moment, the very inability of workers to unite on the basis of a workers' identity thus forms the fundamental limit of struggle. But that limit is at once the dynamic potential of this cycle of struggles, bearing within itself the abolition of gender relations and all other fixed distinctions. It is no historical accident that the end of the former cycle of struggles coincided with a revolt against the primacy of the Worker – a revolt in which feminism played a major role. To re-imagine a workers' movement that would not demote women, blacks, and homosexuals to a subordinate position is to think a workers' movement that lacks precisely the unifying/excluding trait that once allowed it to move at all. With the benefit of hindsight, it is increasingly clear that if the working class (as a class of all those without direct access to means of production) was destined to become the majority of society, the workers' movement was unlikely to organize a clear majority from it. The revolution as communization does not solve this problem, but it takes it onto a new terrain. As surveyors of this new landscape, we must assess the present state of the practical movement toward the end of gender relations. We must also expand discussion of this essential communizing measure.

Until recently, the theory of communization has been the product of a small number of groups organized around the publication of a handful of yearly journals. If few of those groups have taken up the task of theorizing gender, it is because most have been wholly uninterested in examining the real basis of the divisions that mark the existence of the working class. On the contrary, they have busied themselves with trying to discover a revolutionary secret decoder-ring, with which they might be able to decipher the merits and shortcomings of past struggles. Thus, most partisans of communization have thought the revolution as an immediate overcoming of all separations, but they arrived at this conclusion through an analysis of *what communization would have to be in order to succeed where past movements failed*, rather than from a focus on the historical specificity of the present.[188]

For this reason, the tendency organized around Théorie Communiste (TC) is unique, and we largely follow them in our exposition. For TC, the revolution as communization only emerges as a practical possibility when these struggles begin to 'swerve' (*faire l'écart*) as the very act of struggling increasingly forces the proletariat *to call into question and act against its own reproduction as a class*. 'Gaps' (*l'écarts*) thereby open up in the struggle, and the multiplication of these gaps is itself the practical possibility of communism in our time. Workers burn down or blow up their factories, demanding severance pay instead of fighting to maintain their jobs. Students occupy universities, but against rather than in the name of the demands for which they are supposedly fighting. Women break with movements in which they already form a majority, since those movements cannot but fail to represent them. And everywhere, the unemployed, the youth, and the undocumented join and overwhelm the struggles of a privileged minority of workers, making the limited nature of the latter's demands at once obvious and impossible to sustain.

In the face of these proliferating gaps in the struggle, a fraction of the proletariat,

in going beyond the demands-based character of its struggle, will take communizing measures and will thus initiate the unification of the proletariat which will be the same process as the unification of humanity, i.e. its creation as the ensemble of social relations that individuals establish between themselves in their singularity.[189]

For TC, the divisions within the proletariat are therefore not only that which must be overcome in the course of the revolution, *but also the very source of that overcoming.* Perhaps that is why TC, alone among theorists of communization, have devoted themselves to an examination of the gender distinction, as it is perhaps the most fundamental divisions within the proletariat.

TC's work on gender is relatively new, especially for a group which has spent the last thirty years refining and restating a few key ideas over and over again. Their main text on gender, written in 2008, was finally published in 2010 (with two additional appendices) in issue 23 of their journal as *Distinction de Genres, Programmatisme et Communisation*. TC are known for their esoteric formulations. However, with some effort, most of their ideas can be reconstructed in a clear fashion. Since their work on gender is provisional, we refrain from lengthy quotations. TC claim that communization involves the abolition of gender as much as the abolition of capitalist social relations. For the divisions which maintain capitalism maintain the gender division and the gender division preserves all other divisions. Still, as much as TC take steps towards developing a rigorously historical materialist theory of the production of gender, they end up doing little more than suture gender to an already existing theory of the capitalist mode of production (to no small extent, this is because they rely largely on the work on one important French feminist, Christine Delphy[190]).

For our context here, TC have a particularly fascinating theory of communization insofar as it is also a periodization of the history of class struggle – which itself corresponds to a periodization of the history of the capital-labor relation. This provides TC with a uniquely historical vantage on the present prospects for communism. Crucially, TC focus on *the reproduction of the capital-labor relation*, rather than on *the production of value*. This change of focus allows them to bring within their purview the set of relations that actually construct capitalist social life – beyond the walls of the factory or office. And the gender relation has always extended beyond the sphere of value production alone.

I. The Construction of the Category 'Woman'

Woman is a social construction. The very category of woman is organized within and through a set of social relations, from which the splitting of humanity into two, woman and man – and not only female and male – is inseparable. In this way, sexual difference is given a particular social relevance that it would not otherwise possess.[191] Sexual difference is given this fixed significance within class societies, when the category of woman comes to be defined by the function that most (but not all) human females perform, for a period of their lives, in the sexual reproduction of the species. Class society thus gives a social purpose to bodies: because some women 'have' babies, all bodies that could conceivably 'produce' babies are subject to social regulation. Women become the slaves of the biological contingencies of their birth. Over the long history of class society, women were born into a world organized only for men – the primary 'actors' in society, *and in particular the only people capable of owning property*. Women thereby became the property of society as a whole.

Because women are by definition not men, they are excluded from 'public' social life. For TC, this circumscription of the women's realm means that not only are their bodies appropriated by men, but also the totality of their activity. Their activity, as much as their very being, is by definition 'private'. In this way, women's activity takes on the character of *domestic labor*. This labor is defined not as work done in the home, but as women's work. If a woman sells cloth in the market, she is a weaver, but if she makes cloth in the home, she is only a *wife*. A woman's activity is thus considered merely as her activity, without any of the concrete determinations it would be given if it were performed by some other, more dignified social entity. The gender distinction man/woman thereby takes on additional significance as public/private and social/domestic.

Is the unpaid labor of women for men, including perhaps their 'production' of children, therefore a class relation, or even a mode of production (as Delphy calls it, the domestic mode of production)? TC defines class society as a relationship between surplus producers and surplus extractors. The social division between these groups is constitutive of the relations of production, which organize the productive forces for the purpose of producing and extracting surplus. Crucially, these relations must have as their product the reproduction of the class relation itself. However, for TC – and we follow them on this point – *each mode of production is already a totality*, and in fact the social relevance of women's role in sexual reproduction changes with the mode of production. That does not mean that relations between men and women are derivative of the relations between the classes. It means rather that *the relations between men and women form an essential element of the class relation* and cannot be thought as a separate 'system', which then relates to the class-based system.

Of course, this discussion remains abstract. The question now becomes, how do we unite our story about women with our story about the succession of modes of production? For TC, *women are the primary productive force* within all class societies, since the growth of the population forms an essential support of the reproduction of the class relation. The augmentation of the population as the primary productive force remains, throughout the history of class society, the burden of its women. In this way, the *heterosexual matrix* is founded on a specific set of material social relations.

However, we should remind ourselves that the special burden of childbirth predates the advent of class society. Historically, each woman had to give birth, on average, to six children – just in order to ensure that two of those six survived to reproduce the coming generations. The chance that a woman would die in childbirth, in the course of her life, was nearly one in ten.[192] Perhaps the insight of TC is that the advent of class society – which saw a massive increase in the size of the human population – hardened the social relevance of these facts. But *even before the advent of class society*, there was never any 'natural' regime of human sexual reproduction. Age at marriage, length of breastfeeding, number of children born, social acceptability of infanticide – all have varied across human social formations.[193] Their variation marks a unique adaptability of the human species.

But we are concerned less with the long history of the human species than with the history of the capitalist mode of production. Wage-labor is fundamentally different from both ancient slavery and feudal vassalage. In slavery, surplus producers have no 'relation' to the means of production. For the slaves are themselves part of the means of production. The reproduction or upkeep of slaves is the direct responsibility of the slave owner himself. For both men and women slaves, the distinction between public and private thus dissolves, since slaves exist entirely within the private realm. Nor is there any question, for the slaves, of property inheritance or relations with the state, such as taxation. Interestingly, there is some evidence that patriarchy was, perhaps for that very reason, rather weak among slave families in the American South.[194] In vassalage, by contrast, the surplus producers have direct access to the means of production. Surplus is extracted by force. The peasant man stands in relation to this outside force as the public representative of the peasant household. Property passes through *his* line. Women and children peasants are confined to the private realm of the village, which is itself a site of both production and reproduction. The peasant family does not need to leave its private sphere in order to produce what it needs, but rather only to give up a part of its product to the lords. For this reason, peasant families remain relatively independent of markets.

In capitalism, the lives of the surplus producers are *constitutively split* between the public production of a surplus and the private reproduction of the producers themselves. The workers, unlike the slaves, are their 'own property': they continue to exist only if they take care of their own upkeep. If wages are too low, or if their services are no longer needed, workers are 'free' to survive by other means (as long as those means are legal). The reproduction of the workers is thus emphatically not the responsibility of the capitalist. However, unlike the vassals, the workers can take care of their own upkeep only if they return to the labor market, again and again, to find work. Here is the essence of the capital-labor relation. What the workers earn for socially performed production in the public realm, they must spend in order to reproduce themselves domestically in their own private sphere. The binaries of public/private and social/domestic are embodied in the wage-relation itself. Indeed, these binaries will only collapse with the end of capitalism.

For if the capitalists were directly responsible for workers' survival – and thus if their reproduction were removed from the private sphere – *then the workers would no longer be compelled to sell their labor-power.* The existence of a separate, domestic sphere of reproduction (where little production takes place unmediated by commodities purchased on the market) is constitutive of capitalist social relations as such. Social activity separates out from domestic activity as the market becomes the mediating mechanism of concrete social labor performed outside of the home. Production for exchange, which was formerly performed inside the home, increasingly leaves the home to be performed elsewhere. At this point the public/private distinction takes on a spatial dimension. The home becomes the sphere of private activity – that is, women's domestic labor and men's 'free time' – while the factory takes charge of the public, socially productive character of men's work.

Of course, women have also always been wage laborers, alongside men, for as long as capitalism has existed. For TC, the gendered nature of women's domestic work determines that their work, even when performed outside of the home, remains merely women's work. It remains, that is to say, wage labor of a particular sort, namely *unproductive or else low value-added labor*. Women tend to work in part-time, low-wage jobs, particularly in services (though of course today, there are at least some women in all sectors of the economy, including among the highest paid professionals). Women often perform domestic services in other people's homes, or else in their offices and airplanes. When women work in factories, they are segregated into labor-intensive jobs requiring delicate hand-work, particularly in textiles, apparel and electronics assembly. Likewise, work done in the home remains women's work, even if men perform it – which, largely, they do not.

In this sense, once gender becomes embodied in the wage-relation as a binary public/private relation, TC cease to theorize its ground in the role that women play in sexual reproduction. The fact that women's work is of a particular character outside the home is merely true by analogy to the character of the work they perform in the home. It bears no relation to the material ground of women's role in sexual reproduction, and in that sense, it is more or less ideological. By the same token, TC increasingly define the work that women do in the home by its character as the daily reproductive labor performed necessarily outside of the sphere of production – and not by relation to the role that women play in childbirth, as the 'principal force of production'. If, within the capitalist mode of production, women are and have always been both wage-laborers and domestic laborers, why do they remain almost entirely *female*? As TC begin to discuss capitalism, they phase out their focus on sexual reproduction, which disappears under a *materially unfounded* conception of domestic labor (though their references to biology return later, as we will see).

This oversight is a serious mistake. The sexual segregation of work in the capitalist mode of production is directly related to the temporality of a woman's life: as the bearer of children, the main source of their nourishment at young ages (breastfeeding), and their primary caretakers through puberty. Over the long history of capitalism, women's participation in the labor market has followed a distinct 'M-shaped' curve.[195] Participation rises rapidly as women enter adulthood, then drops as women enter their late 20s and early 30s. Participation slowly rises again as women enter their late 40s before dropping off at retirement ages. The reasons for this pattern are well known. Young women look for full-time work, but with the expectation that they will either stop working or work part-time when they have children. When women enter childbearing years, their participation in the labor force declines. Women who continue to work while their children are young are among the poorer proletarians and are super-exploited: unmarried mothers, widows and divorcées, or women whose husbands' incomes are low or unreliable. As children get older, more and more women return to the labor market (or move to full-time work), but at a distinct disadvantage in terms of skills and length of employment, at least as compared to the men with whom they compete for jobs.[196]

For all these reasons, capitalist economies have always had a special 'place' for women workers, as workers either not expected to remain on the job for very long or else as older, late entrants or re-entrants into the labor force. Beyond that, women form an important component of what Marx calls the 'latent' reserve army of labor, expected to enter and leaving the workforce according to the cyclical needs of the capitalist enterprises. The existence of a distinctive place for women in the labor force then reinforces a society-wide commitment to and ideology about women's natural place, both in the home and at work. Even when both men and women work, men typically (at least until recently) earn higher wages and work longer hours outside the home. There thus remains a strong pressure on women, insofar as they are materially dependent on their husbands, to accept their subordination: to not 'push too hard'[197] on questions of the sexual division of labor within the home. Historically, this pressure was compounded by the fact that women were, until after World War II, *de facto* if not *de jure* excluded from many forms of property ownership, making them reliant on men as mediators of their relation to capital. Therefore, women did not possess the juridical freedoms that male proletarians won for themselves – and not for *their* women. Women were not truly 'free' labor in relation to the market and the state, as were their male counterparts.[198]

II. The Destruction of the Category 'Woman'

Though TC fail to explain the ground of the construction of women in capitalism, they do have a provocative theory of how women's situation within capitalism changes according to the unfolding contradictions of that mode of production. 'Capitalism has a problem with women' because, in the present period, *the capital-labor relation cannot accommodate the continued growth of the labor force.* As we have already noted, capital increasingly faces a large and growing surplus population, structurally excessive to its demands for labor. The appearance of this surplus population has coincided with a transformation in the way that capitalist states, the workers' movement, and also feminists have viewed women as the 'principal productive force'. In an earlier moment birth-rates declined precipitously in Europe and the former European settler-colonies. The response was 'pro-natalism'. Civilization supposedly faced imminent degeneration, since women were no longer fulfilling their duty to the nation; they had to be encouraged back into it. By the 1920s, even feminists became increasingly pro-natalist, turning maternalism into an explanation for women's 'equal but different' dignity as compared to men. By the 1970s, however – as the population of poor countries exploded while the capitalist economy entered into a protracted crisis – maternalism was largely dead. The world was overpopulated with respect to the demand for labor. Women were no longer needed in their role as women. The 'special dignity' of their subordinate role was no longer dignified at all.

However, that is only half the story. The other half is to be found in the history of the demographic transition itself, which TC fail to consider. In the course of its early development, capitalism increased workers' consumption and thereby improved their health, reducing infant mortality. Falling infant mortality in turn reduced the number of children that each woman had to have in order to reproduce the species. At first, this transformation appeared as an increase in the number of surviving children per woman and a rapid growth of the population. Thus, the spread of capitalist social relations was everywhere associated with an *increase* in women's reproductive burden. However with time, and now in almost every region of the world, there has been a subsequent reduction, both in the number of children each woman has and in the number of children who subsequently survive infancy and early childhood. Simultaneously, as both men and women live longer, less of women's lifetimes are spent either having or caring for young children. *The importance of these facts cannot be overestimated.* They explain why, in our period, the straight-jacket of the heterosexual matrix has had its buckles slightly loosened, for men as well as women (and even, to a small extent, for those who fit neither the categories of gender distinction, nor those of sexual difference).[199]

As with everything else in capitalism, the 'freedom' that women have won (or are winning) from their reproductive fate has not been replaced with free-time, but with other forms of work. Women's supposed entrance into the labor force was always actually an increase in the time and duration of women's already existing participation in wage-work. But now, since women are everywhere spending less time in childbirth and child-rearing, there has been a reduction in the M-shaped nature of their participation in labor-markets. Women's situation is thus increasingly split between, on the one hand, the diminishing but still heavy burden of childbearing and domestic work, and on the other hand, the increasingly primary role in their lives of wage-work – *within which they remain, however, disadvantaged.* As all women know, this situation expresses itself as a forced choice between the promise a working life supposedly equal to men and the pressure, as well as the desire, to have children. That some women choose not to have children at all – and thus to solve this dilemma for themselves, however inadequately – is the only possible explanation of the fall in the birth rate below what is predicted by demographic transition theory. Fertility is now as low as 1.2 children per woman in Italy and Japan; almost everywhere else in the West it has fallen below 2. In the world as a whole, fertility has fallen from 6 children per woman in 1950 to around 2.5 today.

In this situation, it becomes increasingly clear that women have a problem with markets, *since markets are incompatible with women*. This incompatibility comes down to two facts about the capitalist mode of production. First, capital cannot, if it is to remain capital, take direct responsibility for the reproduction of the working class. It is because workers are responsible for their own upkeep that they are forced to return, again and again, to the labor market. At the same time, labor markets, if they are to remain markets, must be 'sex-blind'.[200] Markets have to evaluate the competition between workers without regard to any non-market characteristics of the workers themselves. These non-market characteristics include the fact that *half of all of humanity is sexed female*. For some employers, sexual difference cannot but appear as an additional cost. Women workers are able to bear children and thus cannot be relied on not to have children. For other employers, sexual difference appears as a benefit *for precisely the same reason*: women provide flexible, cheap labor. Women are thus relegated by capitalist relations – precisely because markets are sex-blind – to women's wage-work.

This incompatibility of women and markets has plagued the women's movement. Feminism historically accepted the gendered nature of social life, since it was only through gender that women could affirm their identity as women in order to organize on that basis. This affirmation became a problem for the movement historically, *since it is impossible to fully reconcile gender – the very existence of women and men – with the simultaneous existence of the working class and capital*.[201] As a result, the women's movement has swung back and forth between two positions.[202] On the one hand, women fought for equality on the basis of their fundamental sameness with respect to men. But whatever the similarity of their aptitudes, women and men are not and never will be the same *for capital*. On the other hand, women have fought for equality on the basis of their 'difference but equal dignity' to men. But that difference, here made explicit as motherhood, is precisely the reason for women's subordinate role.

The workers' movement promised to reconcile women and workers beyond, or at least behind the back of, the market. After all, the founding texts of German Social Democracy, in addition to Marx's *Capital*, were Engels' *Origins of the Family, Private Property and the State*, and Bebel's *Woman and Socialism*. Through struggle, the workers' movement promised to bring women out of the home and into the workforce, where they would finally become the true equals of men. In order to achieve this real equality, the workers movement would socialize women's reproductive work 'after the revolution'. Both housework and childcare would be performed collectively by men and women together. As it became clear to the most extreme elements of the Radical Feminist movement in the 1970s, these measures would never suffice to actually ensure 'real equality' between men and women workers. The only possibility of achieving an equality of workers, at the intersecting limit of both gender and labor, would be *if babies were born in test-tubes, finally having nothing to do with women at all.*[203]

In fact, the workers' movement betrayed its women as soon as it had the chance. Whenever they came close to power, male workers were fully willing to demonstrate their capacity to manage the economy by showing that they, too, knew how to keep women in their place. In the British Communist Party, freeing husbands from domestic work was the main task of women's 'party work'.[204] How could it have been otherwise? Within a world defined by work – or more precisely, by productive labor (a category of capitalism) – women would always be less than men. The attempt to 'raise' women to the equals of men was always a matter of *adjusting a 'universally' relevant movement of workers to fit the 'particular' needs of its women*. The attempt to do so, within the bounds of capitalism, amounted to a minimal socialization of childcare, as well as the institution of a minimal set of laws protecting women from their disadvantages in markets (that is to say, maternity leave, etc). Workers' movements could have gone further along this road. They could have made women more of a priority than they did. But the fact is that they did not. And now, it's over.

The death of the workers' movement has been considered in other texts.[205] Its death marks also the passage from one historical form of revolution to another. Today, the presence of women within the class struggle can only function as a rift (*l'ecart*), a deviation in the class conflict that destabilizes its terms. *That* struggle cannot be *their* struggle, even if, in any given case, they form the majority of the participants. For as long as proletarians continue to act as a class, the women among them cannot but lose. In the course of struggle, women will, therefore, come into conflict with men. They will be criticized for derailing the movement, for diverting it from its primary goals. But the 'goal' of the struggle lies elsewhere. It is only from within this (and other) conflicts that the proletariat will come to see its class belonging as an external constraint, an impasse which it will have to overcome in order to be anything at all beyond its relation to capital. That overcoming is only the revolution as communization, which destroys gender and all the other divisions that come between us.

11

Black Box, Black Bloc
Alexander R. Galloway

Of all the revivals in recent years – a period of history in which the revival itself has been honed to such a degree that it persists as mere 'blank parody' – the revival of Hegel is the most startling, although certainly not for those involved. Hegelianisms of all shapes and sizes prevail today, from Catherine Malabou's dutiful reconstruction of the 'plastic' dialectical transformations, to the hysterical antimaterialism of Slavoj Žižek and his convocation of the inescapable bind between the 'determinate negation' and the 'wholly Other,' from which explodes the terror of proletarian power. Is not Woody Allen's character Alvy Singer in *Annie Hall* the perfect summation of Žižek's political project: *Okay I'm a bigot, but for the left!* Or consider the unrepentant Hegelian Alain Badiou who stakes everything on being as a pure formalism that only ever realizes itself through the event, an absolute departure from the state of the situation.

Only the Hegelian dialectic, and not the Marxist one, can snap back so cleanly to its origins like this, suggesting in essence that *Aufhebung* was always forever a spectralization and not a mediation in general, that in other words the ultimate truth of the Hegelian dialectic is spirit, not negation or becoming or anything so usefully mechanical. The negation is thus *revoked* during synthesis, much more than it is resolved. This would be one way to read the current intellectual landscape, as so many revoked materialisms, so many concepts too terrified by matter to matter.

And so the question comes again, always again: is the dialectic a medium, or does the dialectic demonstrate the absolute impossibility of any kind of mediation whatsoever? What is the status of the obscure, of negation, of the dark corners of being that are rarely ever subsumed by dialectical becoming, or even strategically excluded from it?

Where are we now? In an essay from 2001, the French collective Tiqqun speaks of what they call the cybernetic hypothesis: '[A]t the end of the twentieth century the image of steering, that is to say management, has become the primary metaphor to describe not only politics but all of human activity as well.'[206] The cybernetic hypothesis is, in Tiqqun's view, a vast experiment beginning in the overdeveloped nations after World War II and eventually spreading to swallow the planet in an impervious logic of administration and interconnectivity. 'The cybernetic hypothesis is thus a political hypothesis, a new fable... [It] proposes that we conceive of biological, physical and social behaviour as both fully programmed and also re-programmable.'[207]

The essay is interesting not so much for Tiqqun's description of the late twentieth century, a description of cybernetic society that has become increasingly common today. Rather it is interesting for how the collective describes the appropriate political response to such a hypothesis. They speak of things like panic, noise, and interference. They propose counterstrategies of hypertrophy and repetition, or as they put it 'to execute *other* protocols.'[208]

Yet there is always a strategic obscurantism in their proscriptions, what Tiqqun calls here 'invisible revolt.' 'It is invisible because it is unpredictable to the eyes of the imperial system,' they write, lauding the virtues of mist and haze: '*Fog is the privileged vector of revolt ... Fog makes revolt possible.*'[209]

Invisibility is not a new concept within political theory. But what I would like to explore here is a specific kind of invisibility, a specific kind of blackness that has begun to permeate cybernetic societies, and further that this blackness is not simply an effect of cybernetic societies but is in fact a necessary precondition for them.

The black box: an opaque technological device for which only the inputs and outputs are known. The black bloc: a tactic of anonymization and massification often associated with the direct action wing of the left. Somehow these two things come together near the end of the twentieth century. Is there a reason for this?

Close your laptop tight and what do you see? A smooth outer opaque shell, hiding and housing a complex electronic machine within. With the lid down, there is little with which to interact. Pick it up, put it down, not much more. Open it again and see the situation reversed: now concave, the external surface of the machine is no longer opaque and smooth, rather it is plastered over with buttons and sockets, speakers and screens, boxes and windows, sliders and menus, clicks and drags, taps and double taps. Splayed open, the box begs to be touched, it exists to be manipulated, to be *interfaced*.

There are two kinds of black boxes. The first is the *cipher* and the second is the *function*. With the lid closed the laptop is a black box cipher. With the lid up, a black box function.

The black box cipher was very common during modernity. Marx articulated the logic cleanly in *Capital, vol. 1* with his description of the commodity as having both a 'rational kernel' and a 'mystical shell.' It is a useful device for Marx, portable and deployable at will whenever the dialectic needs to be triggered. Thus the commodity is a black box cipher, but so is value, and so is the relationship between exchange and production, ditto for the class relation, and on and on. Superimpose the cipher and begin to decode. This is the 'rational kernel, mystical shell' logic at its most pure: untouched, the phenomena of the world are so many ciphers, so many mystical black boxes waiting to be deciphered to reveal the rationality (of history, of totality) harboured within.

The black box cipher is similar to Leibniz's monad. Like the monad, the cipher 'has no windows.' It is a cloaked node with no external connectivity. Think again of the laptop with its lid closed. The case is a turtle shell designed to keep out what is out and keep in what is in. This is what the commodity is, to be sure, but it is also what the sign is, what spectacle is, and what all the other cultural phenomena are that model themselves after the commodity logic. Interiority is all; interface is but a palliative decoy, a flourish added for people who need such comforts.

But this is only one half of the story, a half that has served quite nicely for decades but nevertheless needs to be supplemented because, quite simply, the mode of production itself is now a new one with new demands, new systems, and indeed new commodities.

If it could speak today, the black box would say:

'Let us reconnect to the noisy sphere where everything takes place on the surface and in full view of everyone, for this is the plane of production, on whose threshold is already encoded a million mantras for the new economy: "Do what feels right." "Reach out and touch someone." "Play hard." "Don't be evil."'

Fortified with a bright array of windows and buttons, the monad ceases to be a monad. It is still the old cipher, only now it has an interface. It is a cloaked node, one whose external connectivity is heavily managed.

No Future?

Consider how a function works in computer languages, or an API (application programming interface), or a network socket. What is consistent across all these technologies is the notion that visibility should be granted, but only selectively and under stricture of specific grammars of action and expression.

While its conceptual origins go back to Marx and the nineteenth century, the term 'black box' enters discourse proper in the 1940s via military tech slang. Seeking the origins of the black box, Philipp von Hilgers recalls the year 1940 and the Battle of Britain, particularly the transport out of the country of some of Britain's technical secrets via the so-called Tizard Mission. An emergency wartime diplomatic expedition, the Tizard Mission arrived in Washington, DC on September 12, 1940 carrying vital items packaged inside of a black, metal box with the hopes that American scientists could assist their British allies in developing new technologies for the war effort.[210] Inside the black box was another black box, the magnetron, a small microwave-emitting tube suitable for use in radar equipment, which had been modified in recent years from a transparent glass housing to an opaque, and therefore 'black,' copper housing.

On a small scale the magnetron was a black box that allowed the Allies greater flexibility with their radar, but on a larger scale the confrontation of the war itself was a veritable black-box theatre in which enemy objects and messages were frequently intercepted and had to be decoded. The new sciences of behaviourism, game theory, operations research, and what would soon be called cybernetics put in place a new black-box epistemology in which the decades if not centuries old traditions of critical inquiry, in which objects were unveiled or denaturalized to reveal their inner workings – from Descartes's treatise on method to both the Kantian and Marxian concepts of critique to the Freudian plumbing of the ego – was replaced by a new approach to knowledge, one that abdicated any requirement for penetration into the object in question, preferring instead to keep the object opaque and to make all judgements based on the object's observable comportment. In short the behaviourist subject is a black-boxed subject. The node in a cybernetic system is a black-boxed node. The rational actor in a game theory scenario is a black-boxed actor.

Warren McCulloch describes the black box at a meeting in Princeton during the winter of 1943-1944 attended by Norbert Wiener, Walter Pitts and others:

> [We] were asked to consider the second of two hypothetical black boxes that the allies had liberated from the Germans. No one knew what they were supposed to do or how they were to do it. The first box had been opened and [it] exploded. Both had inputs and outputs, so labelled. The question was phrased unforgettably: 'This is the enemy's machine. You always have to find out what it does and how it does it. What shall we do?'[211]

War planes often contained technologies such as radar that should not fall into the hands of the enemy. To avoid this, such technological devices were often equipped with self-destruction mechanisms. Thus when McCulloch says, in this hypothetical scenario, that the first black box exploded he is referring to the fact that its self-destruction mechanism had been triggered. Box number two remained intact, and no telling if there would ever be a chance to capture additional boxes with which to experiment. Thus no attempt could be made to explore the innards of the second box, least risk a second explosion. Any knowledge to be gained from the second box would have to be gained purely via non-invasive observation. The point here is that because of these auto-destruct mechanisms, it was inadvisable if not impossible to open up devices (black boxes) gleaned from the enemy. The box must stay closed. The box must stay black. One must concentrate exclusively on the outside surface of the box, its inputs and outputs.

This is but one historical vignette, of course, yet as this new epistemological framework developed via what, following Norbert Wiener, Peter Galison calls the Manichean sciences and what Tiqqun calls the Cybernetic Hypothesis (cybernetics, operations research, behaviourism, neutral nets, systems theory, cellular automata, game theory, and related disciplines), it became more and more clear that the black box was not simply an isolated device. The black box grew to become a constituent element of how entities and systems of entities were conceived. '[T]he cybernetic philosophy was premised on the opacity of the Other,' writes Galison. 'We are truly, in this view of the world, like black boxes with inputs and outputs and no access to our or anyone else's inner life.'[212]

It is thus today no longer a question simply of the enemy's black box, but the black boxing of the self, of any node contained in a network of interaction. The enemy's machine is not simply a device in a German airplane, it is ourselves: a call center employee, a card reader at a security check point, a piece of software, a genetic sequence, a hospital patient. The black box is no longer a cipher waiting to be unveiled and decoded, it is a function defined exclusively through its inputs and outputs.

Is this the death of Freud and Marx and hermeneutics in general? At the very least one might say that Marx's principle for the commodity has finally come full circle. Today instead of Marx's famous rational kernel in the mystical shell, one must comes to grips with a new reality, *the rational shell and the mystical kernel*, for our skins are already tattooed, our shells are keyboards, our surfaces are interactive interfaces that selectively allow passage from the absolutely visible exterior to the absolutely opaque interior. The shell is rational, even as the kernel remains absolutely illegible. These new black boxes are therefore labelled *functions* because they are nothing but a means of relating input to output, they articulate only their exterior grammar, and black box their innards. Computer scientists quite proudly, and correctly, call this technique 'obfuscation.' 'Function' black boxes include the computer, the protocol interface, data objects, and code libraries. RFC 950 on subnetting procedures puts this principle quite well:

'each host sees its network as a single entity; that is, the network may be treated as a "black box" to which a set of hosts is connected.'[213] This new industrial scenario is one in which a great premium is placed on interface, while interiority matters very little, assuming of course that everything is in its place and up and running. These black boxes have a purely functional being; they do not have essences or transcendental cores.

This is why one must invert the logic of Marx's famous mandate to 'descend into the hidden abode of production.' In other words, and to repeat: It is no longer a question of illuminating the black box by decoding it, but rather that of functionalizing the black box by programming it. To be clear, the point is not to ignore the existence of the new black sites of production, from *maquiladoras* to PC rooms. On the contrary, these black sites are part and parcel of the new industrial infrastructure. The point instead is to describe the qualitative shift in both the nature of production, and perhaps more importantly, the nature of the consumer, for only by describing this new structural relationship can we begin to speak about the structure of critique. In other words, if Marx's 'descend into the hidden abode of production' was an allegory for critique itself, what is the proper allegory for critique today? If neither the descent into production nor the illumination of hiddenness are viable options, what's left?

From the student occupations at the New School, to the political tracts circulating through the University of California, to Tiqqun and the Invisible Committee and other groups, there is a new political posture today, a new political bloc with an acute black-box profile.

The new mantra is: *we have no demands*. We don't want political representation. We don't want collective bargaining. We don't want a seat at the table. We want to leave be, to leave *being*. We have *no* demands.

The power behind the 'no demands' posture is precisely that it makes no claim about power at all. Instead it seeks to upend the power circuit entirely via political nonparticipation. It would be wrong to cast this aside using the typical epithets of cynicism or nihilism, or even to explain it away using the language of state power versus terrorism, which we should remember is the language of Lenin just as much as it is the language of Bush, Obama, Sarkozy, and all the rest, for the key to this new political stance is in its subtractivism vis-à-vis the dimensions of being.

Are we not today at the end of a grand declension narrative beginning over a century ago from time to space and now to appearance itself? Is not the nineteenth and early twentieth century the moment in which time enters western thought, only to be supplanted after World War II by space as a new organising principle? We can speak therefore first of an aesthetics and politics of time, back to Hegel and Darwin and Marx to be sure, but also achieving central importance in the work of Bergson and Heidegger, even Benjamin with his interest in nostalgia and reproduction, or Einstein's scientific treatment of time, or the great 1900 media (as Kittler calls them), the phonograph, the cinema, and all the other temporally serial recorders of empirical inputs. The subsequent breakthrough of structuralism then was not so much the elaboration of the linguistic structure, but the synchronic as such, the anti-temporal, a development so startling that it must only be balanced and recuperated with an equally temporal counterpart in the diachronic.

Nevertheless if the earlier phase introduced a politics of time, the post-war period ushered in a new politics of space. So by the 1970s and '80s we hear of 'situations' and 'geographies,' of 'territorialization's' and 'lines of flight,' of 'heterotopias' and 'other spaces,' of 'nomadic' wanderings and 'temporary autonomous zones,' fuelled in part by Henri Lefebvre's landmark *The Production of Space* (1974). And indeed it was Jameson who put forward the notion that postmodernism is not simply a historical periodization but quite literally the *spatialization* of culture, and hence his more recent call for a reinvention of the dialectic itself, not as a so-called engine of history, but as an engine of spatiality, a 'spatial dialectic.'[214]

This dimensional subtractivism, from time to space, leads to a third step, the politics of the singular dimension. Binary in nature, it reduces all politics to the on/off logic of appearance and disappearance. These are of course the stakes of any periodization theory whatsoever, not so much to assert that computers have taken over, or even the old vulgar economist truism that the so-called computer revolution is less the rise of computing as a new industrial vanguard but the wholesale reorganization of *all* sectors of industry around these new digital devices such that agriculture and logistics and medicine and what have you are now equally computerized, but that a certain kind of logic (binary, supplementarity, multiplicity, etc.) has come to be associated with a certain historical incarnation of the mode of production. The perverse irony, if we can call it that, is that today's binary is ultimately a false binary, for unlike the zeros and ones of the computer, which share a basic numeric symmetry at the level of simple arithmetic, the binaries of offline and online are so radically incompatible that they scarcely interface at all, in fact the 'interface' between them is defined exclusively through the impossibility of interfacing: the positive term carries an inordinate amount of power while the negative term carries an extreme burden of invisibility and alterity. Today's politics then is a kind of rampant 'dark Deleuzianism' in which affirmation of pure positivity and the concomitant acceptance of the multiple in all its variegated forms (Deleuze's univocal being as the absolutely singular One, populated with infinite multiplicities) results nevertheless in the thing it meant to eradicate: a strict binarism between us and them, between the wired world and the dark continents, between state power and the terrorists. The 'no demands' posture flies in the face of all of this.

Again, the proposition: the politics of the new millennium are shaping up to be a politics not of time or of space but of appearance. So instead of Debord or Jameson or Lefebvre a new radical syllabus is shaping up today: Virilio's *The Aesthetics of Disappearance*, Lyotard's *The Inhuman*, or Levinas's *On Escape*. Instead of a politicization of time or space we are witnessing a rise in the politicization of absence – and presence – oriented themes such as invisibility, opacity, and anonymity, or the relationship between identification and legibility, or the tactics of nonexistence and disappearance, new struggles around prevention, the therapeutics of the body, piracy and contagion, informatic capture and the making-present of data (via data mining).[215] It is no coincidence that groups like Tiqqun use anonymous umbrella names for their practice. Here is the Invisible Committee on the superiority of tactics of opacity over tactics of space:

> For us it's not about *possessing territory*. Rather, it's a matter of increasing the density of the communes, of circulation, and of solidarities to the point that the territory becomes unreadable, opaque to all authority. We don't want to occupy the territory, we want to *be* the territory.[216]

The question here is very clearly *not* one of territorial 'autonomy' (Hakim Bey) or a reimagining of space (the Situationists), but rather a question of opacity and unreadability. As McKenzie Wark writes in his fine book *A Hacker Manifesto*, 'There is a politics of the unrepresentable, a politics of the presentation of the nonnegotiable demand.'[217] Strictly speaking then, and using the language of ontology, it is not simply that a new 'cultural logic' has been secreted from the mode of production than it is a claim about logic itself (a logic of logic), for logic is the science of appearing, just as ontology is the science of being. And to be neat and tidy about things, we ought to remember that these new digital devices are all logic machines to begin with.

Tracking this current from the higher attributes downward, which is to say from time to extension (space) to ontics (presence/existence), I shall indulge in that most dismal science of prediction, at my own peril to be sure. Sequentially speaking, then, after ontics comes ontology. So in the future, near or far, one might expect to see a new politics of being, that is to say not simply a politics of durational or historical authenticity or territorial dominance or even identification and appearance, but quite literally a newfound struggle over what is and what can be. Substitute prevention with *preemption*. Substitute the activist mantra 'no one is illegal' with 'no *being* is illegal.' Not just skirmishes over the politics of the body (which in the overdeveloped world have been evacuated to nothingness by all the limp affectivists with their body modifications and designer pharmaceuticals), but struggles over the politics of being. This will not resemble the twentieth-century critiques around essentialism and antiessentialism, for postfordism put an end to that discussion once and for all, leaving us wondering whether we really want what we wished for. It will be a materialist politics to be sure, but also at the same time an immaterial or idealist war in which that old spectre of the 'thought crime' will certainly rear its ugly head again, and people will be put in jail for ideas and forms and scripts and scriptures (which is already happening in and around the new regime of digital copyright and the aggressive policing of immaterial property rights). And perhaps the future is already here, as the 'source fetishists' are already running rampant, be they the champions of the open source movement, or those bioprospecting for new genetic sources deep within the Amazon jungle, or those mining for consumer essences deep within the Amazon web site.

What this means for criticism is another question altogether. The determining aspect of the dialectic today is not so much contradiction as such or synthesis or negation or even the group of terms related to becoming, process, or historicity, but rather that of the asymmetrical binary, a binary so lopsided that it turns into a kind of policed monism, so lopsided that the subjugated term is *practically nonexistent*, and that synthesis itself is a mirage, a mere pseudo technique floated with the understanding it will be recouped, like a day trader floating a short term investment. As Godard famously said: 'this is not a just image, this is just an image.' So if anything can be learned from the present predicament it might be that a *practical nonexistence* can emerge from a being that is practically nonexistent, that subtractive being ($n - 1$) might be the only thing today that capitalism cannot eventually co-opt.

No Future?

To end, we shall not say that there is a new blackness. We shall not ratify the rise of the obscure and the fall of the transparent. But do not decry the reverse either. Simply withdraw from the decision to ask the question. Instead ask: what is this eternity? What is this black box – this black bloc – that fills the world with husks and hulls and camouflage and crime? Is it our enemy, or are we on the side of it? Is this just a new kind of nihilism? Not at all, it is the purest form of love.

Contributors

Jasper Bernes

is a PhD student at UC Berkeley. His dissertation, *The Work of Art in the Age of Deindustrialization*, examines the restructuring of the labor process during the 1960s and 1970s from the point of view of experimental poetry and conceptual art. He is the author of a book of poems, *Starsdown*.

John Cunningham

is a writer based in London who has contributed to *Mute magazine*. His research interests include contemporary ultra-left and post-autonomist theory, environmentalism and the representation of production and wage labor in contemporary cinema.

Endnotes

is a communist theoretical journal produced by a discussion group of the same name based in Britain and the US. It emphasises open-ended enquiry, but core threads so far have been the theory of communization, the Marxian critique of political economy and recent developments in value-form theory and 'systematic dialectic'.

Alexander R. Galloway

is an author and programmer. He is a founding member of the software collective RSG and creator of the Carnivore and Kriegspiel projects. He is author of three books including *The Exploit: A Theory of Networks* (Minnesota, 2007), written in collaboration with Eugene Thacker. Most recently he is cotranslator (with Jason Smith) of *Introduction to Civil War* (Semiotext(e), 2010) by the French collective Tiqqun.

Maya Andrea Gonzalez

is a revolutionary Marxist Feminist from the Bay Area.

Anthony Iles

is a writer and editor preoccupied with noise, art, film, work, housing, urban planning and fiction. He is a contributing editor to *Mute* and occasional teacher at Det Jyske Akademie in Aarhus.

Leon de Mattis

is the author of *Mort à la démocratie* (L'Altiplano, 2007), and was a contributor to the French journal for communization, 'Meeting'.

Benjamin Noys

teaches at the University of Chichester and his most recent work is *The Persistence of the Negative: A Critique of Contemporary Cultural Theory* (2010). His research traverses the field of critical theory, and particularly its intersections with cultural production.

Nicole Pepperell

is Program Director for the Social Science (Psychology) program at RMIT University in Melbourne, Australia, where she is also Lecturer in Social Theory for the school of Global Studies, Social Science, and Planning. Her research interests include Marx and Marxism, immanent social critique, the philosophy of history, and the relationship between changes in everyday practices and the development of novel political ideals and theoretical categories.

Théorie Communiste

is a French journal founded in 1977. Setting out from a critique of the struggles of the late 1960s-early 1970s and the Dutch-German and Italian communist lefts, the journal has worked on overcoming a conception of the revolution and of communism as the liberation of labor and the affirmation of the proletariat. The reworking of the concept of exploitation as the historical course of the contradiction between classes leads to a characterisation of the restructuring of the capitalist mode of production following the crisis of the 1970s as a cycle of struggles which bears communization as its overcoming. That is, the abolition of classes and genders in the production of immediate inter-individual relations.

Alberto Toscano

is senior lecturer in Sociology at Goldsmiths. He is the author of *The Theatre of Production* (Palgrave, 2006) and *Fanaticism: The Uses of an Idea* (Verso, 2010), and a member of the editorial board of *Historical Materialism*.

Marina Vishmidt

is a writer active mainly in the fields of contemporary art, philosophy and political economy. She is doing a PhD at Queen Mary, University of London on speculation as a mode of production.

Evan Calder Williams

is a theorist and graduate student in Santa Cruz, California. He is the author of *Combined and Uneven Apocalypse* (Zero Books, 2011).

Notes

Introduction

[1] See Endnotes, 'What are we to do?' and Leon de Mattis's 'Reflections on the Call', in this collection, for 'communizing' critiques of Tiqqun on these grounds.

[2] Gilles Deleuze and Félix Guattari, *A Thousand Plateaus*, trans. and intro. Brian Massumi (Minneapolis: University of Minnesota Press, 2005), pp.413-415.

[3] Karl Marx, *Capital vol. 1*, intro. Ernest Mandel, trans. Ben Fowkes (Harmondsworth: Penguin, 1976), pp. 941-1084; for the distinction between formal and real subsumption see pp. 1019-1038.

[4] For the emphasis on the continuing co-existence of formal and real subsumption see Endnotes, 'The History of Subsumption', *Endnotes* 2 (April 2010): 130-152, http://endnotes.org.uk/articles/6.

[5] See E. P. Thompson, *The Making of the English Working Class* [1963] (London: Penguin, 1991) for this argument.

[6] This was presciently explored in Michel Foucault's lectures on biopolitics (actually on neoliberalism) given between 1978 and 1979, and now published as Michel Foucault, *The Birth of Biopolitics: Lectures at the Collège de France, 1978-79*, trans. Graham Burchell (Basingstoke: Palgrave, 2008).

[7] For the debate between TC and Dauvé and Nesic on this point see the collection of texts in *Endnotes* 1 (October 2008), http://endnotes.org.uk/issues/1.

[8] Gilles Deleuze, 'Postscript on the Societies of Control' [1990], *October* 59 (Winter 1992): 3-7.

[9] 'How can the proletariat, acting strictly as a class of this mode of production, in its contradiction with capital within the capitalist mode of production, abolish classes, and therefore itself, that is to say: produce communism?', TC, quoted in *Endnotes*, 'The History of Subsumption', p.152.

[10] Théorie Communiste, 'The Glass Floor', riff-raff, http://www.riff-raff.se/wiki/en/theorie_communiste/the_glass_floor.

[11] Jorge Luis Borges, *Collected Fictions*, trans. Andrew Hurley (London: Pen-

guin Books, 1998), pp. 263-264.

[12] Tiqqun, 'Call', http://www.bloom0101.org/call.pdf.

What are we to do?

[13] See for example the collection *After the Fall: Communiqués from Occupied California*, http://afterthefallcommuniques.info/.

[14] The following discussion will focus specifically on are The Invisible Committee, *The Coming Insurrection* (Los Angeles, CA: Semiotext(e), 2009) http://tarnac9.wordpress.com/texts/the-coming-insurrection/ and The Invisible Committee, *Call* (2004), http://www.bloom0101.org/call.pdf, rather than other works associated with Tiqqun, since it is these texts that have been the most influential in the current Anglophone reception of 'communization'. It is primarily with this reception that we are concerned, rather than any more general assessment of Tiqqun as, for example, a contributor to 'continental philosophy'.

[15] For a fuller discussion of these issues, see 'Misery and Debt', and 'Crisis in the Class Relation' in *Endnotes* 2 (April 2010), http://endnotes.org.uk/issues/2.

[16] For a discussion of the concept of programmatism, see Theorié Communiste, 'Much Ado About Nothing', *Endnotes* 1: Preliminary Materials for a Balance Sheet of the Twentieth Century (October 2008): 154-206, http://endnotes.org.uk/articles/13.

[17] 'Plato could well have refrained from recommending nurses never to stand still with children but to keep rocking them in their arms; and Fichte likewise need not have perfected his passport regulations to the point of 'constructing', as the expression ran, the requirement that the passport of suspect persons should carry not only their personal description but also their painted likeness.' Hegel, *Elements of the Philosophy of Right*, p.21.

[18] See, for example, *The Coming Insurrection*, p.101: 'All milieus are counter-revolutionary because they are only concerned with the preservation of their sad comfort'. They protest too much.

[19] Of course, Tiqqun distinguish their approach from the 'leftist' problem-atic of 'what is to be done?' because they see this as denying that 'the war has

already begun'. Instead, the direct question to be posed for Tiqqun is 'how is it to be done'? But we are not merely concerned with this question as literally posed by Tiqqun. The 'what should we do?' in question is that of the post-anti-globalization impasse itself, an impasse which – as we shall see – structures the theoretical content of texts such as *Call* and *The Coming Insurrection*.

[20] By 'alternative' and 'alternativism' here, we refer to practices which aim to establish liberated areas outside of capitalist domination, grasping this as possible independently of, and prior to, any communist revolution. Countercultural milieus in general can be said to be 'alternativist'.

[21] For an excellent critique of the position of the Batko group see Per Henriksson, 'Om Marcel Crusoes exkommunister i Intermundia. Ett bidrag till kommuniseringsdiskussionen', *Riff-Raff* 9 (March 2011), http://riff-raff.se/texts/sv/om-marcel-crusoes-exkommunister-i-intermundia; English translation forthcoming.

[22] *The Coming Insurrection*, pp.29-34.

[23] *The Coming Insurrection*, pp.33-32.

[24] *Call*, p.4.

Communization in the Present Tense

[25] For China and India to manage to constitute themselves as their own internal market would depend on a veritable revolution in the countryside (i.e. the privatisation of land in China and the disappearance of small holdings and tenant farming in India) but also and above all on a reconfiguration of the global cycle of capital, supplanting the present globalization (i.e. this would mean a renationalization of economies, superseding / preserving globalization, and a definancialization of productive capital).

[26] These examples are mostly French; publication of this text in Britain and the United States provides an opportunity to test the theses that are defended here.

[27] It is a crisis in which the identity of overaccumulation and of under-consumption asserts itself.

[28] '(T)hat thing [money] is an objectified relation between persons (...) it is

262

objectified exchange value, and exchange value is nothing more than a mutual relation between people's productive activities.' Marx, *Grundrisse* (Harmondsworth: Penguin, 1973), p. 160.

Reflections on the Call

[29] Presented at 'Meeting 2' (2005). The original French text available here: http://meeting.communisation.net/archives/meeting-no-2/les-textes-publies-6/article/reflexions-autour-de-l-appel.

[30] '*Call*' was published by The Invisible Committee in 2004, references in the text are given to the English translation available here: http://www.bloom0101.org/call.pdf.

[31] Gilles Dauvé and Karl Nesic, 'Communization: a "call" and an "invite"', Troploin 4 (September 2004), http://troploin0.free.fr/ii/index.php/textes/19-communisation-un-appel-et-une-invite. Dauvé concludes his text by writing: 'If the situation corresponds to that described by those preparing *Meeting* and those who've published *Call*, the simple concomitance of the two projects should inspire at the very least a reciprocal interest among their respective participants. To our knowledge this is not the case.' He also adds, in relation to *Call*: 'Whatever reservations we can hold, this text manifests an existence, an experience, in particular in the anti-globalization actions of recent years.' It is necessary to point out here that the 'concomitance' of these projects has nothing fortuitous about it, and that the 'experience' which *Call* represents can also be found in Meeting. Certain articles of *Meeting* 1 and *Call* concern strictly the same topics.

[32] The expressions 'area which poses the question of communization', 'communizing movement' and 'communizing current' are used in the sense that I respectively gave them in *Meeting* 1 ('Three Theses on Communization'). The 'communizing current' designates the theoretical groups which explicitly employ the concept of communization as an important pole of their reflection (this current being admittedly relatively restricted for the moment). 'The area which poses the question of communization' incorporates a much larger part of the present and past proletarian movement. It characterizes those moments of the class struggle where the central problematic was something close to what one could at present understand by communization: in short, how to realize the immediacy of social relations. That which signals the

existence of this area is the crystallization around the communizing question at a given moment in a given struggle, without thinking that this portion of the proletariat could exist separately or perpetuate itself beyond the class struggle in general. Finally the 'communizing movement' is something to be created. Debates must be provoked in the midst of this area – in the struggles and the moments where the communizing problematic seems to appear – to form a movement which will make this demand explicit in the heart of these struggles.

³³ Translators note: in French radical circles the terms 'l'alternatif' and 'alternativisme' designate the activity of those who believe it possible to fulfill their desire for change within capitalist society, alongside the mainstream in an alternative or countercultural world – a kind of third, 'drop out', option between reform and revolution. The terms are translated throughout by 'alternative'.

³⁴ Dauvé, op.cit.

³⁵ There will be an exchange of blows with the cops, a few broken windows and cameras, some trashed hotel lobbies and many trashed brothels in the city center – and also a lot of arrests, some trials (including one protester sentenced to a four-month stretch) and an order of the Prefecture of the Rhine which banned all demonstrations in the city center.

³⁶ Leon de Mattis, 'Trois thèses sur la communisation', *Meeting* 1 (2004), http://meeting.communisation.net/archives/meeting-no-1/les-textes-publies/article/trois-theses-sur-la-communisation.

³⁷ Translators note: *Call* capitalizes the two French versions of 'we', nous and on, in order to highlight the distinction between the 'we' of the party (NOUS) from the more abstract and impersonal 'we' of society / the citizen (ON).

³⁸ Translators note: Heidegger's term for inauthentic being, 'Das Man', is generally translated into English as 'the They', although it is more literally rendered by its French translation 'le On' (the one). The common usage of 'on' to mean 'we' (a little like the 'royal we', but for commoners) thus allows for a Heideggerian distinction which is not translatable into German or English.

³⁹ I talk of 'questions' because every practice, in this type of struggle, is an attempt to respond to a particular problem.

[40] Tiqqun, *Tout a failli, vive le communisme!* (Paris: La Fabrique, 2009).

[41] For a very useful, and charmingly acerbic, survey of the ultra-Left varieties of this phenomenon, as viewed in retrospect from the perspective of communization theory, see (Roland Simon/Chemins non tracés) *Histoire critique de l'ultra-gauche.* Trajectoire d'une balle dans le pied (Paris: Éditions Senonevero, 2009).

[42] Negri's vitriol against the PCI, and Badiou's against the PCF, are among the more obvious examples.

[43] On the idea, drawn from Badiou's writings of the 1980s, of an 'expatriation' of Marxism, see my 'Marxism Expatriated: Alain Badiou's Turn', in *Critical Companion to Contemporary Marxism* (Leiden: Brill, 2008), pp. 529-48.

[44] Rosa Luxemburg, 'Reform or Revolution', in *Rosa Luxemburg Speaks*, ed. Mary-Alice Waters (New York: Pathfinder Press, 1970), pp. 51-128.

[45] See *Histoire critique de l'ultra-gauche.*

[46] Theorié Communiste, 'Communization in the Present Tense' (this volume).

[47] Endnotes, 'Communisation and Value Form Theory', *Endnotes* 2 (April 2010), p. 95.

[48] See the whole of the first issue of Endnotes for the documents of the debate between the invariant-humanist (Gilles Dauvé and Karl Nesic of Troploin) and historical-anti-humanist (TC) wings of communization theory, *Endnotes* 1 (2008), http://endnotes.org.uk/issues/1.

[49] Daniel Bensaïd, 'Stratégie et politique: de Marx à la 3e Internationale', in *La politique comme art stratégique* (Paris: Éditions Syllepse, 2010), p. 73.

[50] For some recent and relevant work on this, see Ching Kwan Lee, *Against the Law: Labor Protests in China's Rustbelt and Sunbelt* (Berkeley: University of California Press, 2007).

[51] See especially Neil Smith, *Uneven Development: Nature, Capital and the Production of Space*, third edition (London: Verso, 2010) and David Harvey, *Spaces of Global Capitalism: Towards a Theory of Uneven Geographical*

Development (London: Verso, 2006).

52 I've tried to explore the present relevance of this problematic in 'Dual Power Revisited: From Civil War to Biopolitical Islam', *Soft Targets*, 2.1 (2006).

53 'The immediate economic element (crises, etc.) is seen as the field artillery which in war opens a breach in the enemy's defences – a breach sufficient for one's own troops to rush in and obtain a definitive (strategic) victory, or at least an important victory in the context of the strategic line. Naturally the effects of immediate economic factors in historical science are held to be far more complex than the effects of heavy artillery in a war of maneuver, since they are conceived of as having a double effect: 1. they breach the enemy's defences, after throwing him into disarray and causing him to lose faith in himself, his forces, and his future; 2. in a flash they organize one's own troops and create the necessary cadres – or at least in a flash they put the existing cadres (formed, until that moment, by the general historical process) in positions which enable them to encadre one's scattered forces; 3. in a flash they bring about the necessary ideological concentration on the common objective to be achieved. This view was a form of iron economic determinism, with the aggravating factor that it was conceived of as operating with lightning speed in time and in space. It was thus out and out historical mysticism, the awaiting of a sort of miraculous illumination.' Antonio Gramsci, *Selections from the Prison Notebooks* (London: Lawrence & Wishart, 1971), p. 487.

54 For these arguments, see Roland Simon, *Le Démocratisme radical* (Paris: Éditions Senonevero, 2001).

55 See for example Carl Boggs, 'Marxism, Prefigurative Communism, and the Problem of Workers' Control', *Radical America* 11.6 (1977) and 12.1 (1978).

56 See Peter Thomas's excellent *The Gramscian Moment: Philosophy, Hegemony and Marxism* (Leiden: Brill, 2009).

57 On a purely theoretical rather than strategic plane, see the stimulating reflections on the uses of dead labor in Moishe Postone, *Time, Labor and Social Domination: A reinterpretation of Marx's critical theory* (Cambridge: Cambridge University Press, 1993), p. 361.

58 'The proper management of constituted environments ... may therefore

require transitional political institutions, hierarchies of power relations, and systems of governance that could well be anathema to both ecologists and socialists alike. This is so because, in a fundamental sense, there is nothing unnatural about New York city and sustaining such an ecosystem even in transition entails an inevitable compromise with the forms of social organization and social relations which produced it'. David Harvey, *Justice, Nature and the Geography of Difference* (Oxford: Blackwell, 1996), p. 186. See also Harvey's important recent intervention, 'Organizing for the Anticapitalist Transition', *Interface: a journal for and about social movements*, 2 (1): 243 - 261 (May 2010), available at: http://interfacejournal.nuim.ie/wordpress/wp-content/uploads/2010/11/Interface-2-1-pp243-261-Harvey.pdf.

[59] I speak of necessary alienation (or necessary separation) by analogy with Marcuse's distinction between necessary and surplus repression in *Eros and Civilization*.

[60] I've discussed this in terms of the question of equality, and commensuration through value, in 'The Politics of Abstraction: Communism and Philosophy', in Costas Douzinas and Slavoj Žižek (eds.), *The Idea of Communism* (London: Verso, 2010). The key textual references are Marx's 'Critique of the Gotha Programme' and Lenin's gloss on it in *State and Revolution*.

Capitalism: Some Disassembly Required

[61] Karl Marx, *Grundrisse: Foundations of the Critique of Political Economy (Rough Draft)*, trans. M. Nicolaus (Harmondsworth: Penguin Books, 1973), p.159.

[62] Georg Lukács, 'Reification and the Consciousness of the Proletariat', in *History and Class Consciousness: Studies in Marxist Dialectics*, trans. R. Livingstone (London: Merlin Press, 1971), p.83.

[63] Max Horkheimer and Theodor W. Adorno, *Dialectic of Enlightenment: Philosophical Fragments*, trans. E. Jephcott (Stanford, CA.: Stanford University Press, 2002).

[64] Christopher J. Arthur, *The New Dialectic and Marx's Capital* (Leiden; Boston: Brill, 2004).

[65] Moishe Postone, *Time, Labor and Social Domination: A Reinterpretation of*

Marx's Critical Theory (Cambridge: Cambridge University Press, 1993).

[66] Karl Marx, *Capital: A Critique of Political Economy, Volume One*, trans. B. Fowkes (London: Penguin Books in association with New Left Review, 1990) pp.173-5.

[67] Marx, *Capital*, p.175 n35.

[68] Ibid., p.90.

[69] Ibid., p.102.

[70] Ibid., p.125-6.

[71] Ibid., p.126.

[72] Ibid., pp.121-6.

[73] Cf. Eugen von Böhm-Bawerk, *Karl Marx and the Close of His System* (London: T.F. Unwin, 1898), chp. 4.

[74] Marx, *Capital*, p.138.

[75] Ibid., pp.138-63.

[76] Francis Wheen, *Marx's Das Kapital: a Biography* (Vancouver: Douglas & McIntyre, 2007), p.42.

[77] Dominick LaCapra, *Rethinking Intellectual History: Texts, Contexts, Language* (Ithaca: Cornell University Press, 1983), p.333.

[78] Marx, *Capital*, pp.151-2.

[79] Ibid., pp.151-2.

[80] Ibid., p.168.

[81] Ibid., pp.166-8.
[82] Ibid., p.179.

[83] Ibid., pp.421-2.

[84] Ibid., pp.678-82.

[85] Ibid., pgs. 716, 724; cf. also Karl Marx, 'Results of the Immediate Process of Production', in *Capital*, pp.949-53.

[86] Marx, *Capital*, p.255.

[87] Ibid., p.256.

[88] Ibid., p.255.

[89] Cf. Thomas T. Sekine, *An Outline of The Dialectic of Capital* (New York: St. Martin's Press, 1997).

[90] Marx, *Capital*, p.199.

[91] Postone, *Time, Labor and Social Domination*.

[92] Marx, *Capital*, p.200.

[93] Ibid., p.152.

[94] Ibid., p.133.

Work, Work Your Thoughts, and Therein see a Siege

[95] The two primary accounts we are referring to are: John Roberts, 'Introduction: Art, "Enclave Theory" and the Communist Imaginary', *Third Text* 23:4 (2009): 353-367, and Stewart Martin, 'Artistic Communism –a sketch', *Third Text*, 23: 4(2009): 481-494.

[96] Endnotes, 'Misery and Debt', *Endnotes* 2 (2010): 20-51, http://endnotes.org.uk/articles/1.

[97] Endnotes, 'Communization and Value-form Theory', *Endnotes* 2 (2010): 68-105, http://endnotes.org.uk/articles/4, p.88.

[98] Ibid., p.103.

[99] Karl Marx, *Capital Vol.1*, Trans. Ben Fowkes (London: Penguin, 1990), p.548.

[100] Endnotes, 'Crisis in the Class Relation', *Endnotes* 2 (2010): 2-19, http://endnotes.org.uk/articles/2, p.19.

[101] Maria Gough, *The Artist as Producer: Russian Constructivism in Revolution* (Berkeley and Los Angeles: California University Press, 2005).

[102] John Roberts, 'Productivism and Its Contradictions', *Third Text* 23.5 (September 2009), p.528.

[103] Boris Arvatov, 'Everyday Life and the Culture of the Thing (Toward the Formulation of the Question)', trans. Christina Kiaer, in *October* 81 (Summer 1997), p.121.

[104] We are indebted here to Nicholas Thoburn's research on the 'communist object' which brings Arvatov and Benjamin into dialogue. Nicholas Thoburn, Communist Objects and the Values of Printed Matter (London: Objectile Press, 2010), reprinted from *Social Text* 28.2 (Summer 2010).

[105] Roberts, 2009.

[106] Martin, 2009, p.482.

[107] 'Conversation with Maurizio Lazzarato June 23, 2010 – Public Editing Session #3, in Exhausting Immaterial Labor in Performance Joint issue of *Le Journal des Laboratoires* and *TkH Journal for Performing Arts Theory* 17 (October 2010).

[108] Stewart Martin, 'The Pedagogy of Human Capital', *Mute*, 2.8 (April 2008), http://www.metamute.org/en/Pedagogy-of-Human-Capital. This discussion clarifies the importance of keeping the two principal concepts of 'autonomy' – that of art's autonomy in capitalism which was developed by Theodor Adorno, and the autonomy of the working class as developed by the 'workerist' communism of 1970s Italy – analytically and practically distinct.

[109] Comte de Saint-Simon, La Politique quoted in Margaret A. Rose, *Marx's Lost Aesthetic*, (Cambridge: Cambridge University Press, 1984), p.12.

[110] Ibid., p.12.

[111] Comte de Saint-Simon, On Social Organization quoted in Margaret A. Rose, Ibid., p.13.

[112] Diedrich Diedrichsen, 'Audio Poverty', http://e-flux.com/journal/view/143.

[113] Mike Cooley, *Architect or Bee?: the human / technology relationship* 2nd Edition (London: The Hogarth Press, 1987), p.65.

[114] Karl Marx, 'The Value-Form', Appendix to the 1st German edition of *Capital, Volume 1*, http://www.marxists.org/archive/marx/works/1867-c1/appendix.htm.

[115] Marx, Ibid.

[116] Karl Marx, *Contribution to a Critique of Political Economy*, http://www.marxists.org/archive/marx/works/1859/critique-pol-economy/ch01.htm.

[117] Moishe Postone, *Time, Labor and Social Domination: a reinterpretation of Marx's critical theory* (Cambridge: Cambridge University Press, 1993).

[118] Karl Marx, 'Draft of an Article on Friedrich List's book: Das Nationale System der Politischen Oekonomie I' (1845) http://www.marxists.org/archive/marx/works/1845/03/list.htm.

[119] Bruno Astarian, 'Crisis Activity & Communization', *Mute Magazine* (2011), http://www.metamute.org/en/news_and_analysis/crisis_activity_communisation.

[120] Theodor Adorno, *Aesthetic Theory*, trans. Robert Hullot-Kentor (London: Continuum, 2007), p.55.

[121] Ibid.

[122] Paulo Virno, 'The Dismeasure of Art. An Interview with Paolo Virno' http://classic.skor.nl/article-4178-nl.html?lang=en.

[123] This specific relationship between financialization and art is explored in detail in Melanie Gilligan, *Notes on Art, Finance and the Un-Productive Forces* (Glasgow: Transmission Gallery, 2008), http://www.transmissiongallery.org/files/Publication/GI_2008.pdf.

[124] John Roberts, *The Intangibilities of Form* (London and New York: Verso, 2008), p.209.

[125] Virno, 'The Dismeasure of Art'.

[126] Astarian, 2011.

[127] Adorno, 2007, p.53.

[128] Giorgio Agamben, *The Man Without Content*, trans. Georgia Albert (Stanford University Press, Stanford, 1999), p.35.

[129] 'The condition of the development of the forces of production as long as they requires an external spur, which appears at the same time as their bridle.' Karl Marx, *Grundrisse* (London: Penguin, 1993), p.415.

[130] Marx, *Grundrisse*, p.421.

[131] Théorie Communiste, 'The Present Moment', Sic 1.1 (n.d.), http://sic.communization.net/en/the-present-moment.

[132] Ibid.

[133] Théorie Communiste, 'Self-organization is the first act of the revolution; it then becomes an obstacle which the revolution has to overcome', *Revue Internationale pour la Communization* (2005), http://meeting.communization.net/spip.php?page=imprimir_articulo&id_article=72.

[134] Ibid.

[135] The best introduction to the ideas of Théorie Communiste and the context from which they emerge can be found in the conversation between Aufheben and TC in 'Communist Theory: Beyond the Ultra-left', *Aufheben* 11 (2003), http://libcom.org/library/beyond-ultra-left-aufheben-11 and in the introduction and afterword to *Endnotes* 1 (2008), http://endnotes.org.uk/issues/1.

[136] Théorie Communiste, 'Le plancher de verre', in Les Emeutes en Grèce (Senonevero, 2009). English translation here: http://www.riff-raff.se/wiki/en/theorie_communiste/the_glass_floor.

[137] Ibid. The translation of écart as swerve here capture only part of the meaning. Since écart also means 'gap' we are meant to understand this phrase as implying that acting as a class, under such conditions, entails a certain distance (or gap) from oneself, thus putting one's identity into question. Elsewhere TC identify theory as itself the product of the gap created by new forms of class struggle.

[138] Ibid.

[139] 'Reality is an Illusion, Normality is Beyond US', ed. *Occupied London, A*

Day When Nothing is Certain: Writings on the Greek Insurrection, p.14, http://www.occupiedlondon.org/blog/wp-content/uploads/2009/11/a-day-when-nothing-is-certain.pdf.

[140] Guy Debord, *The Society of the Spectacle* (Cambridge, Mass: Zone Books, 1995).

[141] http://wewanteverything.wordpress.com/2009/09/24/communique-from-an-absent-future/.

[142] See the following account of the Wheeler occupation, which attempts to read the day as an example of 'care' just as much as antagonism, Amanda Armstrong and Paul Nadal, 'Building Times: How Lines of Care Occupied Wheeler Hall', *Reclamations* 1 (December 2009), http://reclamationsjournal.org/issue01_armstrong_nadal.html. See also, for one of the most trenchant reflections on this problem, the section 'Living-and-Fighting', from Tiqqun, *This is Not a Program* (Semiotext(e), 2011).

[143] Théorie Communiste, 'Who We Are', (n.d.), http://theoriecommuniste.communization.net/English/Presentation,17/Who-we-are

Fire to the Commons

[144] 'The commons' may be understood as a material organization, point of condensation, and resource/support structure, of a community.

[145] Other than any position that could utter phrases about the emancipatory potential of either YouTube or the sort of desperate networks of informal labor in slums: to affirm this is utter stupidity.

[146] Original title in French is *Capital et Gemeinswesen*. English translation by David Brown, from which passages are drawn, is available online at: http://www.marxists.org/archive/camatte/capcom/index.htm.

[147] Camatte's definition of 'proletarianization', in the 1970 remarks to *Capital and Community*, is simply 'formation of those without reserves.'

[148] The well-known passage from Marx, which forms the basis of this investigation, can be found in *Grundrisse*, pp.225-226; references throughout are from: *Grundrisse: Foundations of the Critique of Political Economy (Rough Draft)*, trans. Martin Nicolaus (New York: Penguin Books, 1973).

[149] Note: in the discussion that follows, I guard the specifically gendered term 'man' that Marx and Camatte use. This is in part for consistency with the texts I am discussing, but more in order to draw a terminological distinction. Namely, I use 'man' to signal the discussion of a figure particular to capital and the history of its theorization (man as labor power and attendant potential 'rights'), in which 'man' stands in for a restricted notion of what counts as 'our common essence,' with the particular pitfalls of essentializing and the dominant historical figuration of the worker (especially the revolutionary worker) as specifically male. Conversely, I use 'human' to describe a wider field of the species. In other words, to say that 'man is time's carcass' is to speak specifically of the dominant notion of 'man' and the material practices that aim to reduce the entire range of human experience to that restricted zone.

[150] Camatte himself, in *Capital and Community*, points to a reading of labor power as the 'real content of man': 'Democracy is comparison par excellence. However, its standard is abstract man, while the real content of man – labor-power – enters into the economic movement.'

[151] Marx *Grundrisse*, p.324.

[152] Ibid., pp.452-435.

[153] The 'without reserves' (senza-riserve) and the universal class are Bordigist concepts employed by Camatte. The former is juxtaposed to the mistaken notion of the 'reserve army of labor' and functions as a way to understand the production of surplus populations with nothing to fall upon and which cannot be adequately 'incorporated' by capital. The universal class is an extension of this notion to include the 'new middle classes' – those who are a 'representation of surplus value' – in a version of a proletarianization thesis.

Make Total Destroy

[154] Walter Benjamin, 'The Destructive Character', in *One Way Street* (London and New York: Verso, 1998), p.157.

[155] Make Total Destroy Facebook Page, http://www.facebook.com/group.php?gid=43581396610.

[156] Gilles Dauvé and Francois Martin, T*he Eclipse and Re- Emergence of the Communist Movement* [1974] (London, Antagonism Press, 1997), p.36.

[157] Jacques Camatte, 'The Wandering of Humanity', in *This World We Must Leave* (New York: Autonomedia, 1995), p.56.

[158] Camatte, 1995, p.118.

[159] Walter Benjamin, 'Critique of Violence', in *One Way Street* (London and New York: Verso, 1998), p.153.

[160] John Cunningham, 'Invisible Politics', *Mute Magazine* 14.2 (2009), p.48; http://www.metamute.org/en/content/invisible_politics.

[161] See *Endnotes* 1 (2008), http://endnotes.org.uk/issues/1, for the debate between Theorié Communiste and Troploin.

[162] Endnotes, 'Afterword', *Endnotes* 1 (2008): 208-216, http://endnotes.org.uk/articles/14, p. 212.

[163] Alain Badiou, Destruction, Negation, Subtraction, (2007), http://www.lacan.com/badpas.htm.

[164] Alain Badiou, *Theory of the Subject*, trans. Bruno Bosteels (London and New York: Continuum, 2009), p.131.

[165] Alain Badiou, *The Century*, trans. Alberto Toscano (Cambridge: Polity, 2007).

[166] Étienne Balibar, 'Reflections on Gewalt', *Historical Materialism* 17.1 (2009): 99-125, p.109.

[167] Quoted in Theorié Communiste, The Glass Floor, http://libcom.org/library/glass-floor-theorie-communiste.

[168] Benjamin, 'Critique of Violence', p.149.

[169] See Alberto Toscano, 'Real Abstraction Revisited', http://www.le.ac.uk/ulmc/research/cppe/pdf/toscano.pdf

[170] Luca Basso, 'The Ambivalence of Gewalt in Marx and Engels: On Balibar's Interpretation', *Historical Materialism*, 17.2 (2009): 215-236, p.220.

[171] Moishe Postone, *Time, Labor and Social Domination* (Cambridge: Cambridge University Press, 1996), p.281.

[172] Théorie Communiste, The Glass Floor.

[173] Michael Denning, 'Wageless Life', *New Left Review* 66 (2010), p.79.

[174] See 'Misery and Debt', *Endnotes* 2 (2010): 20-51, http://endnotes.org.uk/articles/1, for an analysis of the tendency towards a population surplus to the requirements of capital.

[175] Benjamin, 'Critique of Violence', pp. 145-6.

[176] Benjamin, 'Critique of Violence', p. 144.

[177] Théorie Communiste, *Self-organization is the first act of the revolution; it then becomes an obstacle which the revolution has to overcome*, http://libcom.org/library/self-organization-is-the-first-act-of-the-revolution-it-then-becomes-an-obstacle-which-the-revolution-has-to-overcome.

[178] Giorgio Agamben, 'In Praise of Profanation', in *Profanations* (New York: Zone Books, 2007), p.86.

[179] Théorie Communiste, *Self-organization is the first act of the revolution*.

[180] Bruno Astarian, 'Crisis Activity and Communization', http://libcom.org/library/crisis-activity-communisation-bruno-astarian.

[181] Pierre Klossowski in Denis Hollier (ed.), *The College of Sociology 1937-39* (Minneapolis: University of Minnesota Press, 1988), p.418.

[182] Dauvé and Martin, 1997, p.34.

[183] Agamben, 'In Praise of Profanation', p.86.

[184] See Gilles Dauvé (a.k.a. Jean Barrot), Making Sense of the Situationists (1979), for a critique of the Situationists that emphasises this – given that Agamben is influenced by Debord it seems the elision of production in favour of a concentration upon commodification continues in his elaboration of spectacular capitalism.

[185] Théorie Communiste, The Glass Floor.

Communization and the Abolition of Gender

[186] Thanks to Francesca Manning for her invaluable help in working through the ideas in this text. I'd also like to thank Aaron Benanav for his help in editing this piece.

[187] See 'Misery and Debt', *Endnotes* 2 (2010): 20-51, http://endnotes.org.uk/articles/1.

[188] For a key debate on this point, see *Endnotes* 1 (2008), http://endnotes.org.uk/issues/1.

[189] Théorie Communiste, 'The Present Moment', unpublished.

[190] Christine Delphy and Diana Leonard, *Familiar Exploitation* (Cambridge: Polity Press, 1992).

[191] Not all human beings fit into the categories of male and female. The point is not to use the language of biology to ground a theory of naturalized sexuality, as distinct from a socialized gender. Nature, which is without distinction, becomes integrated into a social structure – which takes natural averages and turns them into behavioral norms. Not all 'women' bear children; maybe some 'men' do. That does not make them any less beholden to society's strictures, including at the level of their very bodies, which are sometimes altered at birth to ensure conformity with sexual norms.

[192] These statistics make it clear to what extent violence against women, sometimes carried out by women themselves, has always been necessary to keep them firmly tied to their role in the sexual reproduction of the species. See Paola Tabet, 'Natural Fertility, Forced Reproduction', in Diana Leonard and Lisa Adkins, *Sex in Question* (London: Taylor and Francis, 1996).

[193] For an introduction to demography, see Massimo Livi-Bacci, *A Concise History of World Population* (Malden, Mass. and Oxford: Blackwell, 2007).

[194] Ellen Meiksins Wood, 'Capitalism and Human Emancipation', *New Left Review* I/167 (Jan-Feb 1988): 3-20.

[195] The term comes from Japan, see Makotoh Itoh, *The Japanese Economy Reconsidered* (Palgrave 2000).

[196] Johanna Brenner and Maria Ramas, 'Rethinking Women's Oppression', *New Left Review* I/144 (Mar-Apr 1984): 33-71.

[197] Ibid.

[198] For a more developed theory of women's relation to property, see 'Notes

on the New Housing Question', *Endnotes* 2 (2010): 52-66, http://endnotes.org.uk/articles/3.

[199] The ground of this loosening, as well as its timing, has remained inexplicable within the bounds of queer theory.

[200] Brenner and Ramas, 'Rethinking Women's Oppression'.

[201] In this sense, we are of course interested only in the history of women's situation within the workers' movement. Bourgeois suffragettes argued for property-based voting qualifications – thus excluding women as class enemies. By the middle of the twentieth century, these same bourgeois became defenders of women's maternal role – at the same time as they founded organizations to control the bodies of women among the 'dangerous classes'.

[202] Joan W. Scott, *Only Paradoxes to Offer* (Cambridge, Mass.: Harvard University Press, 1996).

[203] Radical feminism followed a curious trajectory in the second half of the 20th century, taking first childbearing, then domestic work, and finally sexual violence (or the male orgasm) as the ground of women's oppression. The problem was that in each case, these feminists sought an ahistorical ground for what had become an historical phenomenon.

[204] On the history of women's situation within the workers' movement, see Geoff Eley, *Forging Democracy* (Oxford: Oxford University Press, 2002).

[205] Théorie Communiste, 'Much Ado about Nothing', *Endnotes* 1 (2008), http://endnotes.org.uk/articles/13.

Black Box, Black Bloc

[206] Tiqqun, 'L'Hypothèse cybernétique', *Tiqqun* 2 (2001): 40-83, p.44.

[207] Ibid., p.42.

[208] Ibid., p.69, emphasis added.

[209] Ibid., p.73, p. 80. See also Tiqqun's concept of the 'human strike,' particularly in the text 'Comment faire?', *Tiqqun* 2 (2001): 278-285.

[210] Philipp von Hilgers, 'Ursprünge der Black Box', in Philipp von Hilgers

and Ana Ofak (eds.), Rekursionen: Von Faltungen des Wissens (Berlin: Fink, 2009), pp.127-145. For a detailed investigation of the origins and outcomes of cybernetics research in America see Peter Galison, 'The Ontology of the Enemy: Norbert Wiener and the Cybernetic Vision', *Critical Inquiry* 21.1 (Autumn, 1994): 228-266; he discusses black boxes on pp.246-252.

[211] Warren McCulloch, 'Recollections of the Many Sources of Cybernetics', *ASC Forum* 6, n. 2 (Summer, 1974 [1969]): 5–16, p.12.

[212] Galison, 'The Ontology of the Enemy', p.256.

[213] J. Mogul, et al., 'Internet Standard Subnetting Procedure', *RFC 950*, http://www.faqs.org/rfcs/rfc950.html.

[214] Fredric Jameson, *Valences of the Dialectic* (New York: Verso, 2009), pp.66-70.

[215] See John Cunningham, 'Clandestinity and Appearance', *Mute Magazine* 2.16 (2010): 74-87, http://www.metamute.org/en/content/clandestinity_and_appearance.

[216] The Invisible Committee, *The Coming Insurrection* (Los Angeles: Semiotext(e), 2009), p.108.

[217] McKenzie Wark, *A Hacker Manifesto* (Cambridge: Harvard University Press, 2004), p.231.

Minor Compositions

Other titles in the series:

Forthcoming:

As well as a multitude to come…